LEITHS

HOW TO COOK
DESSERTS

JENNY STRINGER   CLAIRE MACDONALD
CAMILLA SCHNEIDEMAN

Photography by Peter Cassidy

Quadrille
PUBLISHING

CONTENTS

NOTES

✳ All spoon measures are level unless otherwise stated:
1 tsp = 5ml spoon; 1 tbsp = 15ml spoon.

✳ Use medium eggs unless otherwise suggested. Anyone who is pregnant or in a vulnerable health group should avoid recipes that use raw egg whites or lightly cooked eggs.

✳ Use fresh herbs unless otherwise suggested.

✳ If using the zest of citrus fruit, buy unwaxed fruit.

✳ Timings are guidelines for conventional ovens. If you are using a fan-assisted oven, set your oven temperature approximately 15°C (1 Gas mark) lower. Use an oven thermometer to check the temperature.

INTRODUCTION

Busy lifestyles and a healthier approach to sugar and fat mean that we now regard puddings as an occasional treat or a way to mark a special occasion rather than an everyday feature in our diet. Taking the time to create a pudding demonstrates a desire to share something special with others, and the fact that it is a frivolous extra makes it all the more fun and delicious.

Puddings give huge pleasure, and there are plenty of enticing options to choose from here. Some of the recipes are incredibly simple and can be prepared quickly: try the quick chocolate and cherry soufflé (see page 61) or a pain perdu with butterscotch apricots (see page 80) when you are short of time. For a family gathering where you have more time to cook, try a classic like summer pudding (see page 26), which is always impressive as you cut into it and remove the first slice. Opt for something more elegant for a special evening dinner, such as caramel pannacotta with nutty croquant (see page 88) or pistachio pavlova with oranges and pomegranate (see page 120).

The success of a pudding is in the detail: the volume of the meringue or the rise of the sponge are not achieved by magic, although sometimes it might seem so. In this book we explain the techniques that have helped our students achieve success. We hope you will find that the tips we have shared during years of teaching in our London school will help you master new skills, give you more confidence in the kitchen and encourage you to make delicious puddings the whole year round.

MAKING THE MOST OF THE SEASONS

Making mouthwatering puddings offers you the opportunity to use the best of the fruit available. Just choose one type of berry in place of another or substitute a different kind of stone fruit (peaches, apricots, plums, cherries, nectarines) according to the season and, of course, your preference. So make the raspberry and cinnamon torte (on page 34) using blackberries when the summer has turned to autumn or the cherry clafoutis (on page 78) with plums when cherries are not so plentiful.

Most fruit can be frozen, whole or in pieces depending on the fruit, or made into a purée and frozen, to add some colourful summer cheer to the winter months. Berries can be frozen whole or puréed; stone fruit will need to be stoned and cut into chunks; rhubarb should be cut into 2cm lengths; and apples and pears should be peeled, cored and cut into chunks. To freeze, place the prepared fruit in a single layer on trays lined with cling film and freeze until solid, then transfer to a freezer bag or lidded plastic container. Open freezing in this way will ensure that the fruit won't freeze together as a solid block. There is no need to defrost the fruit first before adding to crumbles, pies or cakes.

To make a basic fruit purée, place the prepared fruit in a saucepan and add about 50ml water for every 500g fruit. Cook over a low heat until the fruit is soft, then either mash the fruit or purée in a blender, depending on the texture you require. Sweeten the purée with sugar to taste. Allow it to cool and then transfer to plastic containers, seal and freeze.

SUGAR IN PUDDINGS

Most pudding recipes include some sugar to season and sweeten the dish. We say season, as one of the purposes of using sugar is to bring out the flavour of the other ingredients in the recipe, most notably fruit flavours. Add sufficient sugar to a fruit purée and the fruit flavour sings out, but holding back can mean the sourness dominates the taste.

It is also worth thinking about the contrast of sweetness in different elements of a dish. We sweeten the cream for a Pavlova despite the meringue itself being made almost entirely from sugar, because the contrast between the sweet meringue and the unsweetened cream lends the cream an almost savoury or 'cheesy' flavour. Conversely, adding a slightly savoury element to a sweet dish, such as a salted praline with a vanilla ice cream, can add another dimension, enhancing the flavour and transforming the ordinary into something special.

Certainly, from a health perspective, we are all advised to keep an eye on the amount of sugar in our diets. The occasional pudding is less likely to be a problem than the amount of hidden sugar in so much of the food we buy.

It is also possible to experiment with alternative sources of sweetness such as agave syrup, date syrup or rice malt syrup, and use them in place of sugar in dishes, as their lower GI means they do not result in the same 'sugar high' and consequent energy slump associated with refined sugar.

The amount of sugar that is needed to make puddings palatable is certainly a matter of taste, so by all means reduce the sugar in the recipes in this book if you wish, but not too much in those recipes where the chemistry of the dish would be affected, such as meringues, ice creams, sorbets, roulades and sponge puddings.

1
FRUIT PUDDINGS

Fruit, with its natural combination of sugar and acidity, provides a wealth of inspiration to the cook. In late summer, a plate of perfectly ripe figs, drizzled with honey and a spoonful of Greek yoghurt, makes an elegant ending to a Mediterranean meal, and takes little effort. A winter treat of a hot fruit pudding, juices bubbling through a crumble, provides a different kind of satisfaction, and even more so when served with custard or clotted cream.

We love the sheer variety when making fruit puddings; cooking with fruit in season, especially when that season is tantalisingly short, as well as the luxury of using varieties available from all over the world.

Some of these recipes were developed to make the most of a fruit in the short spell it is at its best, such as the ripe cherries needed for the cherry cobbler (see page 32), and some to enjoy a summer glut in a new and delicious way, such as the raspberry and cinnamon torte (see page 34).

SEGMENTING CITRUS FRUIT

Citrus fruit is an essential ingredient in many puddings. The aromatic zest adds depth and contrast, particularly to rich dishes, the juice can be used to make jellies, and the segmented flesh is lovely in fruit salads.

Removing the segments cleanly from citrus fruit, leaving behind the core and membrane, makes the segments much more attractive and more palatable. To catch any juice as you segment the fruit, you can place the board over a lipped tray.

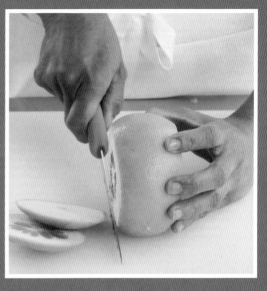

1 Top and tail the fruit, to remove just the ends and no more.

2 Stand the fruit on its end. Using a small, serrated knife, cut off the remaining zest and pith, following the natural curve of the fruit, then trim away any pith left on the fruit.

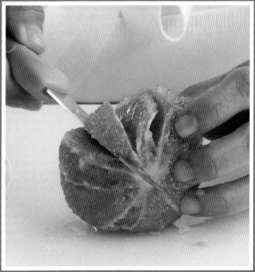

3 Put the fruit on its side on a board. Carefully cut on either side of the membrane dividing the segments to release them and place in a bowl. Once all the segments are removed, squeeze the core and membrane over a bowl, to extract the juice.

ZESTING CITRUS FRUIT

The zest – the very thin outer skin – of citrus fruit, lends a wonderful flavour. It does not include the thick, white, soft pith beneath, which is bitter. If you intend to use the zest, buy unwaxed fruit if you possibly can.

GRATING CITRUS ZEST Use a very fine, sharp grater or fine zesting Microplane, to grate the zest. Avoid digging deeply with the grater or some of the white pith will be removed with the zest, giving a bitter flavour.

Where a recipe calls for the zest of ½ lemon, lime or orange, you will find it easier to zest this quantity from a whole fruit. If the juice is not required for the recipe, wrap the fruit in cling film and keep in the fridge to use another time.

PARING CITRUS ZEST A strip of finely pared citrus zest is sometimes used to lend flavour. Using a swivel peeler, remove a wide, fine strip of zest from an unwaxed lemon (or other fruit), avoiding the bitter pith. If some pith is removed with the zest, use a serrated knife to carefully shave it off from the zest.

CITRUS ZEST JULIENNE To obtain needle-like shards to use for decoration, trim the edges of the zest strips to neaten, then layer on a board and slice into fine julienne. To soften, simmer gently in stock syrup (see page 142) for 3–5 minutes. Remove with a slotted spoon and lay out on baking parchment to dry.

CITRUS FRUIT SALAD IN SPICED CARAMEL

SERVES 4

¼ quantity spiced caramel
    sauce (see page 145,
    using 125g sugar)
2 large oranges

1 yellow or pink grapefruit
4 kumquats
½ small pineapple

The caramel sauce here is flavoured with star anise, coriander seeds and cinnamon, making this the perfect refreshing end to any Asian inspired meal. The syrup is also delicious when poured over a combination of pineapple, orange and mango.

1 Leave the caramel sauce to cool, then cover and refrigerate overnight to allow the flavours to infuse.

2 Prepare the fruit. On a board set over a lipped tray, to catch the juice, peel and segment the oranges and grapefruit, taking care to remove all the pith (see page 10). Slice the kumquats as finely as possible, discarding any seeds. Peel the pineapple, cut out the core and cut the flesh into even chunks, about 2cm. Reserve any juice. Put all the prepared fruit in a serving dish.

3 Stir the reserved fruit juice into the caramel sauce to loosen it. If it has thickened a lot overnight, add a little extra water.

4 Strain the caramel sauce over the fruit, stir in any reserved fruit juice and chill before serving.

Variation

✱ **Pineapple and mango in a lime caramel** Use the lime caramel sauce variation (on page 145) and add 4–6 dried lime leaves, ½ small pineapple, peeled and cut into wedges, and a mango, peeled and sliced off the stone. Leave to macerate in the fridge for 24 hours before serving.

PROSECCO POACHED PEACHES WITH AMARETTI

SERVES 4

6 peaches
1 orange
325g golden caster sugar
750ml Prosecco
1 vanilla pod

FOR THE AMARETTI
85g icing sugar
85g ground almonds

1 egg white
2 tsp amaretto liqueur

AMARETTO CREAM (OPTIONAL)
1 tbsp amaretto liqueur
100ml crème fraîche
Icing sugar, to taste

This is a lovely way to make the most of peaches in season as well as the rather variable 'ripen at home' peaches on sale at supermarkets. Served here with an optional amaretto cream, they are also delicious served with the buttermilk sorbet on page 137.

1 Heat the oven to 180°C/gas mark 4. Line a large baking sheet with non-stick baking parchment.

2 Cut the peaches in half vertically and remove the stones. Finely pare the zest from the orange and squeeze the juice.

3 Put the sugar into a medium saucepan with the Prosecco, orange zest and juice. Heat gently until the sugar has dissolved, stirring occasionally. Split the vanilla pod in half lengthways and add to the pan.

4 Add the peaches to the pan and cover with a dampened cartouche (see page 155) to keep the fruit immersed and hold in the steam. Bring to the boil then turn down to a simmer for 10–25 minutes, or until the peaches are just tender (the time varies considerably depending on the ripeness of the peaches).

5 Once tender, remove the pan from the heat and leave the peaches in the syrup to cool. When they are cool enough to handle, lift them out of the syrup and peel away the skins, then return the peaches to the syrup to finish cooling.

6 Meanwhile, to make the amaretti, sift the icing sugar and ground almonds together into a medium bowl. In a separate bowl, beat the egg white to stiff peaks (see page 109) then carefully fold in the sugar and almond mixture, followed by the amaretto.

7 Place teaspoonfuls of the mixture on the prepared baking sheet, at least 3cm apart to allow for spreading. Bake in the oven for 15–20 minutes until lightly browned. Remove from the oven and leave on the tray for 5 minutes before removing to a wire rack to cool completely.

8 For the amaretto cream, if serving, stir the amaretto into the crème fraîche and sweeten with icing sugar to taste. Serve the poached peaches with their syrup, the amaretti and the amaretto cream, if wished.

HONEY AND THYME ROASTED FIGS

SERVES 4	
12 small, ripe figs	50ml Pedro Ximenez sherry
4 tbsp clear honey	or Marsala
1 thyme sprig	

Pedro Ximenez is a deliciously rich, sweet and fragrant sherry, with a strong flavour of caramelised raisins.

1 Heat the oven to 220°C/gas mark 7.

2 Cut a cross into the figs through the stem end to come three quarters of the way down, so that they are still held together at the base. Squeeze the base of each fig a little to open the quarters out and reveal the inside of the fruit.

3 Arrange the figs in 4 small ovenproof serving dishes, 3 per dish, so they are close together but not squashed. Trickle 1 tbsp of the honey over each trio of figs. Strip the leaves from the thyme sprig and scatter these over the figs, then drizzle over the sherry or Marsala.

4 Bake in the oven for 10–15 minutes, or until the figs are hot, softening and browning on top. Serve warm, with Greek yoghurt if you like.

Variation

✱ Roasted figs with honey and orange Omit the thyme and replace the sherry with the juice of ½ orange.

ROASTED
SUGAR PLUMS

SERVES 4–6

30g unsalted butter
30 Victoria plums
60g soft light brown sugar
75ml rich Madeira

TO SERVE
Vanilla or salted caramel
    ice cream (see page 126)

Victoria plums are easily identified by their small size, distinctive iridescence, purple-red skins and perfumed, golden-yellow flesh. Sadly, their season is short, but the recipe also works well with red or yellow plums, or apricots. Reduce the quantity of regular plums or apricots to 20, as they are larger than Victoria plums.

1 Heat the oven to 200°C/gas mark 6. Melt the butter in a small saucepan over a low heat.

2 Cut the plums in half and remove their stones. Arrange, cut side up, in a single layer in 1 large or 2 small shallow ovenproof dishes, so that they are just touching.

3 Brush the melted butter over the plums, then sprinkle with the sugar. Pour the Madeira around the plums, taking care not to dislodge the sugar.

4 Bake for 15–20 minutes, basting them frequently with the buttery Madeira juices. When cooked, the plums should be tender when pierced with the tip of a sharp knife.

5 Turn the oven off and transfer the cooked plums to a warmed serving dish, using a slotted spoon. Keep them warm in the oven while you reduce the juices.

6 Pour the cooking juices from the dish into a small pan. Place over a medium heat and boil rapidly until thick and syrupy. Spoon over the warm plums and serve with vanilla or salted caramel ice cream.

A note on Madeira...

✳ Madeira is a fortified wine, produced in varying styles, ranging from dry to rich or sweet. This recipe calls for the rich, sweeter variety, which is dark in colour with aromas and flavours of toffee and raisins. Marsala and sweet dessert wines are good substitutes for Madeira.

MUSCAT POACHED PEARS

SERVES 6	
1 lemon	500ml Muscat or Sauternes
500ml water	dessert wine
250g caster sugar	6 pears

Select firm pears to poach. Conference or Packham are the best varieties to use, as they will hold their shape when cooked.

1 Finely pare the zest from the lemon in a long strip and squeeze the juice. Put the water, sugar and lemon zest into a saucepan, just large enough for the pears to stand upright. Place over a low heat and dissolve the sugar; occasional gentle stirring will help this process, but avoid splashing the syrup up the sides of the pan. Add the dessert wine and heat gently.

2 Meanwhile, core the pears using a melon baller; the smaller the melon baller the less pear will be wasted. Start by carefully inserting the melon baller at the base of the pear and removing a little of the pear. Continue to tunnel through, removing a little at a time until the core has been removed, leaving the stalk intact (as shown).

3 Peel the pears using a swivel peeler. Leave the stalk attached and start peeling the pear from the base of the stalk, drawing the peeler down and following the natural curve of the pear (as shown). Take care not to dig too deeply into the flesh. Trim the base of each pear, if necessary, so it can stand upright. If you are not planning to cook the pears immediately, keep them immersed in cold water with the lemon juice added to prevent them from discolouring.

4 To cook, stand the pears upright in the saucepan, ensuring they are covered by the wine and sugar syrup; add a little more water if necessary. If the pears start to float, place a dampened cartouche (see page 155) on top of them, in contact with the sugar syrup (as shown). Increase the heat until an occasional bubble rises to the surface. Maintain this gentle heat and poach the pears until tender, about 20–30 minutes, depending on

the variety and ripeness. When cooked, their colour will have changed from opaque to slightly translucent. To check, carefully lift a pear out of the liquid and insert a cutlery knife a little way in, where you have removed the core; it should meet with minimal resistance.

5 Once the pears are tender, carefully transfer them to the container in which they will be stored or served. Bring the syrup to the boil and reduce to intensify the flavour. Keep tasting the syrup as it reduces and, when you are happy with the flavour and sweetness, leave to cool before pouring over the pears.

6 The pears will keep in the fridge for up to a week. They can be used whole or cut up for use in various recipes.

Variations

✳ **Honey poached pears** For the poaching liquid, use 1 litre water, omitting the dessert wine, and add 200g clear honey.

✳ **Aromatic poached pears** For the poaching liquid, use 1 litre water, omitting the dessert wine, and increase the sugar to 500g. Flavour with the following ingredients individually or in any combination: the finely pared zest of ½ orange; 1 vanilla pod, split lengthways; 1 or 2 cinnamon sticks; 2 star anise; 8–10 cloves.

✳ **Pears poached in red wine** For the poaching liquid, use 1 bottle of good quality red wine, 300g caster sugar and 1–2 cinnamon sticks (or other spices from the suggestions in the variation above).

CARDAMOM POACHED APRICOTS

SERVES 4	
1 orange	150ml sweet dessert wine
100g granulated sugar	6–8 cardamom pods
100ml water	500g apricots

This recipe uses a spiced syrup to infuse the apricots with a subtle flavour of cardamom. You could use a cinnamon stick or a star anise instead if you prefer. The poached apricots can also be frozen, although they will soften a little more when they are defrosted.

1 Finely pare the zest from the orange in a long strip and squeeze the juice. Put the sugar into a medium saucepan with the water and heat gently until the sugar has dissolved, stirring occasionally. Add the dessert wine, orange zest and juice. Crack the cardamom pods and add these to the pan too.

2 Cut the apricots in half and remove the stones. Add the apricots to the sugar syrup and cook over a gentle heat for 5 minutes, or until they are soft but not falling apart. If they are very ripe, take the pan off the heat as soon as the sugar syrup starts steaming.

3 Remove from the heat and set aside to cool. Remove the spices and serve the apricots at room temperature with some of the syrup spooned over. They are lovely with ice cream, crème fraîche or Greek yoghurt.

Variations

✱ **Poached spiced plums** Use plums instead of apricots. Omit the dessert wine, increase the water to 250ml and up the sugar to 200g. Add a vanilla pod, split lengthways, a cinnamon stick and a star anise to the poaching liquid in place of the orange and cardamom. Poach gently for 10 minutes, or until the plums are tender but still keeping their shape. Leave to cool in the syrup and, once cool, remove the vanilla pod and spices.

✱ **Greengages with ginger** Use greengages instead of apricots. Replace the orange and cardamom with a 4cm piece of fresh root ginger, peeled and sliced. Poach the greengages gently for 10 minutes, or until they are tender but still keeping their shape. Remove the ginger slices when the greengages have cooled and stir in 2 pieces of preserved stem ginger, chopped.

A note on poaching...

✱ Poaching is a very gentle method of cooking that allows for the transfer of flavours and ensures that the fruit does not break up during cooking. The liquid is kept below a simmer; a small bubble should only occasionally break the surface.

RHUBARB AND VANILLA COMPOTE

SERVES 4

500g rhubarb (about 2–3
   thick or 4–5 thin stalks)
100ml apple juice or sweet
   dessert wine

100–150g caster sugar,
   to taste
¼–½ vanilla pod

Baking the rhubarb rather than simmering it in a pan is a good way to keep the pieces relatively intact, which looks beautiful (rather than collapsing to a purée), particularly if using the fine stalks of delicately coloured forced rhubarb, which becomes available early in the year.

1 Heat the oven to 200°C/gas mark 6.

2 Trim the ends off the rhubarb, then cut the stalks into 2cm pieces and place in a baking dish, in a single or double layer.

3 Pour the apple juice or wine into a small saucepan, add the sugar and vanilla pod and place over a low heat to dissolve the sugar. Occasional gentle stirring will help this process, but avoid splashing the syrup up the sides of the pan. Once dissolved, bring to a simmer for 1 minute, then pour it over the rhubarb.

4 Bake in the oven for 15–20 minutes, then gently stir the mixture without breaking up the rhubarb. Taste the rhubarb and syrup and sprinkle over a little more sugar if it tastes too sharp. Return to the oven until the rhubarb is tender, but still holding its shape.

5 Remove from the oven and leave the rhubarb to cool in the dish, then discard the vanilla pod. Serve the compote cold or warm with vanilla pannacotta (see page 86) or vanilla ice cream (see page 126).

Variations

✳ **Rhubarb and ginger compote** Omit the vanilla. Proceed as above, then stir in a finely chopped piece of preserved stem ginger, along with 2 tbsp of the syrup from the jar, when the rhubarb has finished cooking. Allow to cool.

✳ **Rhubarb and honey compote** Omit the vanilla and mix 100ml apple juice with 2 tbsp honey (clear or set) and bake as above. Sweeten with more honey or sugar to taste once the rhubarb has finished cooking. Allow to cool.

A note on using vanilla pods...

✳ A vanilla pod, or part of a vanilla pod, should be slit with a knife down its length to allow the flavour to be released. For a more pronounced flavour, scrape out the seeds and add these, along with the scraped-out pod. Used pods can be rinsed under cold running water, dried and put into a jar of sugar to infuse flavour and make vanilla sugar.

SPARKLING SUMMER BERRY COMPOTE

SERVES 4

150g raspberries
150g blackberries
125g strawberries
100g blueberries

100ml Prosecco
25ml Chambord
125g caster sugar
½ vanilla pod

Chambord, a delicious black raspberry liqueur, really enhances the flavour of summer fruits. When added to Prosecco or Champagne, it also makes a lovely cocktail. Alternatively, cassis or crème de mûre work very well in this fresh-tasting berry compote.

1 Place the raspberries in a bowl. Place the blackberries, strawberries and blueberries in a colander and give them a gentle rinse with cold water, then place on kitchen paper to dry.

2 Hull the strawberries and cut them into halves, or quarters if they are large. Place all the fruit in a shallow, heatproof dish.

3 Put the Prosecco, Chambord and sugar into a small saucepan. Scrape out the seeds from the half vanilla pod, then add both the seeds and empty pod to the pan. Heat gently until the sugar is dissolved, stirring occasionally.

4 Bring to the boil and let bubble for 1 minute. Pour the boiling syrup over the fruit, give it a gentle stir to make sure it is all coated in the syrup, then cover the dish with cling film and allow the fruit to sit in the syrup while it cools.

5 Serve the compote slightly warm, or chilled, with a dollop of lightly whipped cream or crème fraîche if you like.

GOOSEBERRY AND ELDERFLOWER COMPOTE

SERVES 4–6

750g fresh gooseberries
50g caster sugar, or to taste
75ml water

2 heads of elderflower or
    3 tbsp elderflower cordial

This is a great compote to make when gooseberries and elderflowers are in season, the flavours being such a classic pairing. However, it also works well if you use frozen gooseberries and elderflower cordial. The acidity of the gooseberries cuts through the richness of a vanilla bavarois or ice cream perfectly.

1 Put the gooseberries, sugar and water in a medium saucepan. Cook over a low heat until the gooseberries release their juices and just begin to pop.

2 Gently wash the elderflower heads, if using, in a bowl of cold water, then tie them in a piece of muslin with string. Add them to the gooseberries (or add the cordial) and simmer very gently for 5 minutes, or until the syrup has thickened enough to coat the back of a spoon.

3 Allow the compote to cool with the muslin bag of elderflowers left in, if using. Taste and add more sugar if necessary.

4 Remove the elderflowers and squeeze any syrup into the compote. Serve at room temperature or slightly chilled.

A note on using frozen fruit...

✱ If using frozen gooseberries, there is no need to add the water when cooking them.

BLACKBERRY AND LEMON COMPOTE

500g blackberries
1 lemon

70g caster sugar, or to taste

A lovely compote to make in the autumn when you can gather blackberries from hedgerows. It is delicious served with steamed puddings, ice creams, creamy mousses and pannacotta.

1 Gently rinse the blackberries and allow them to dry on kitchen paper. Use a swivel peeler to pare strips of zest from the lemon and squeeze the juice of half the lemon.

2 Put the blackberries, sugar, lemon zest and juice in a medium saucepan and cook over a low heat until the berries just release their juices, then simmer very gently until the juices become syrupy and lightly coat the back of the spoon, about 5 minutes.

3 Allow the compote to cool, remove the lemon zest and add more sugar or lemon juice to taste.

Variations

✱ **Blackberry and cinnamon compote** Omit the lemon. Place the blackberries in a pan with the sugar, the juice of 1 orange and a cinnamon stick, broken in half. Cook as above, adding more sugar once cooked to taste. Leave the cinnamon stick in the compote while it cools to extract more of its flavour, but remove before serving.

✱ **Raspberry and lime compote** Swap raspberries for the blackberries and lime for the lemon, simmering for 2–3 minutes only, as raspberries are more delicate and will release their juices as soon as they are heated. A lovely flavour combination that is well worth a try.

SUMMER PUDDING

SERVES 6

1kg mixed soft fruit, such as redcurrants, blackcurrants, blackberries, raspberries and strawberries
150ml water

170g caster sugar, or to taste
10 medium-thick slices of white bread, ideally 1–2 days old

It is important to make this pudding a day in advance, to allow time for the shape to set. You will need a 1 litre pudding basin.

1 Put the fruit, except the strawberries, in a medium saucepan with the water and sugar and cook gently over a low heat for about 5 minutes until the fruit is softening but still has a vibrant colour. Add the strawberries and continue to cook for 2 minutes until the strawberries are just softening. Taste and adjust the sweetness, if necessary.

2 Transfer the fruit to a colander set over a bowl and set aside until most of the juice has drained into the bowl. Press the fruit a little to extract more juice, but avoid crushing it to a pulp.

3 Cut the crusts off all but 2 slices of the bread, and cut in half slightly on the diagonal, but not in triangles. Cut 2 discs from the remaining 2 slices of bread, one to fit in the bottom of the pudding basin and a larger one to cover the top of the basin once filled with fruit. (This top layer will not be seen so you can fill any gaps with bread off-cuts.)

4 Dip the smaller disc of bread in the juice and place in the bottom of the pudding basin. Dip the diagonal pieces of bread in the juice and use them to line the basin, overlapping each piece of bread a little and pressing them together to ensure a good seal.

5 While the fruit is still just warm, spoon it into the bread-lined basin, ensuring the fruit is well packed in to give the pudding a good shape. Dip the larger bread disc in the juice and use to cover the fruit. Stand the pudding basin on a lipped tray, then press a saucer or plate on top of the pudding and put a heavy weight, about 500g, on top. Leave in a cool place overnight to allow the pudding to set in shape.

6 Pour any remaining fruit juice into a saucepan and boil to reduce to a syrupy consistency. Taste and add more sugar if necessary, then leave to cool.

7 When ready to serve, remove the weight and the saucer. Invert a serving dish over the bowl and turn both over together. Give the pudding basin a sharp shake, which should release the pudding, and carefully remove the pudding basin. Spoon the reduced juice over the pudding. Serve with double cream lightly whipped with a little caster sugar to sweeten.

A note on using frozen fruit...

✳ You can use frozen fruit, but reduce the water quantity to 50ml, as it will release more water as it is heated.

A note on unmoulding...

✳ To ensure an easy release, you can line the pudding basin with several layers of cling film before lining it with the bread. After inverting the pudding, carefully peel away the cling film.

PLUM AND ORANGE CRUMBLE

500g plums (about
    10–12 plums)
10g butter, to grease
3–5 tbsp light muscovado
    sugar, to taste
2 oranges

FOR THE CRUMBLE
200g plain flour
Pinch of salt
125g butter
60g light muscovado sugar

Muscovado sugar gives this crumble a lovely biscuity flavour. Taste the plums for sweetness before you cook them – unripe fruit will need more sugar. Ripe plums don't even need to be cooked before topping with the crumble. You will need a 1.2–1.3 litre baking dish.

1 Heat the oven to 200°C/gas mark 6.

2 Halve the plums and remove the stones. Use the butter to grease an ovenproof baking dish. Spread the plums out in the dish and sprinkle with the sugar.

3 Finely grate the zest of one of the oranges, then peel and segment both fruit (see page 10), reserving the segments and catching any juice. Sprinkle the juice over the plums with half of the zest, reserving the rest.

4 Very ripe plums don't need to be pre-baked. If your plums are quite firm, bake them in the oven for 10 minutes, or until they are starting to soften.

5 Meanwhile, to make the crumble, sift the flour and salt into a large bowl. Cut the butter into small cubes and rub it into the flour with your fingertips until the mixture resembles coarse breadcrumbs. Stir in the sugar and the remaining orange zest, and rub in gently to ensure they are evenly distributed through the crumble.

6 Remove the plums from the oven and stir in the orange segments, turning the top layer of plums cut side down. Sprinkle the crumble mixture over the top. Cook in the oven for 30–40 minutes, or until the crumble is lightly browned and the fruit juices are bubbling. Serve hot or warm with ice cream, custard or pouring cream.

Variation

✳ Individual apricot and almond crumbles Cut 12 ripe apricots in half vertically and remove the stones. Divide the apricot halves between 4 ramekins, sprinkle with about ½ tbsp brown sugar and 1 tbsp apple or peach juice and bake for 15–20 minutes, as above. Make the crumble using 75g plain flour, a pinch of salt, 30g ground almonds, 60g butter and 30g caster sugar. Grind 5 amaretti biscuits to a coarse powder in a food processor and stir into the crumble. Top each ramekin with the crumble and bake for 25–30 minutes, or until the crumble topping is brown and the fruit juices are bubbling. Any leftover crumble mix can be frozen.

RHUBARB AND GINGER CRUMBLE

SERVES 4

500g rhubarb (about 2–3
thick or 4–5 thin sticks)
10g butter, to grease
1 small piece of preserved
stem ginger in syrup, plus
2–3 tbsp syrup from the jar
3–5 tbsp soft light brown
sugar, to taste

FOR THE CRUMBLE
200g plain flour
Pinch of salt
½–1 tsp ground ginger
125g butter
60g caster sugar

Here preserved stem ginger is used to add a sweet ginger flavour to the crumble filling. This is a really useful standby ingredient and can be used sliced, along with its syrup, to transform a bowl of vanilla ice cream, or natural or Greek-style yoghurt. For the crumble, you will need a 1.2–1.3 litre baking dish.

1 Heat the oven to 200°C/gas mark 6.

2 Trim the ends off the rhubarb and cut into 3cm pieces. Use the butter to grease an ovenproof dish and place the rhubarb in it.

3 Roughly chop the stem ginger and stir it into the rhubarb with the sugar and the ginger syrup. Set aside.

4 For the crumble, sift the flour, salt and ground ginger into a large bowl. Cut the butter into small cubes and rub it into the flour with your fingertips until it resembles coarse breadcrumbs. Stir in the caster sugar and sprinkle the crumble mixture over the rhubarb.

5 Bake in the oven for 40–50 minutes, or until the rhubarb is soft when prodded with a sharp knife and the crumble is lightly browned. Serve hot or warm with ice cream, custard or pouring cream.

Variations

✱ **Pear and mincemeat crumble** Omit the rhubarb, stem ginger and soft brown sugar. Peel, core and chop 1kg pears into large pieces. Add 3–4 tbsp mincemeat. Proceed as for the main recipe.

✱ **Raspberry and nectarine crumble** Omit the rhubarb, ginger and sugar. Remove the stones from 4 nectarines and cut the fruit into large chunks. Mix with 200g fresh raspberries, adding 1 tbsp caster sugar if the raspberries taste a little sour. Omit the ground ginger from the crumble and use either vanilla sugar instead of the caster sugar, or stir ½ tsp vanilla extract thoroughly through the caster sugar before adding it to the crumble mixture.

✱ **Rosemary and red fruit crumble** Replace the rhubarb and ginger with 500g red fruit, such as raspberries, blueberries, blackcurrants, strawberries and blackberries, adding only 1–2 tbsp caster sugar, depending on tartness. Alternatively, add some chopped peaches to make up the weight or use a bag of frozen forest fruits supplemented with available fresh fruit. Make the crumble as for the main recipe, omitting the ground ginger and stirring 1–2 tsp very finely chopped rosemary into the crumble with the sugar.

GOOSEBERRY OAT CRISP

SERVES 6

50g rolled jumbo oats
4 tbsp apple juice
50g blanched hazelnuts
40g blanched almonds
100g self-raising flour,
   plus extra to dust
Large pinch of ground ginger
Large pinch of ground
   cinnamon
Large pinch of freshly
   grated nutmeg
Pinch of salt
50g butter, plus extra
   to grease

40g demerara sugar, plus
   extra to sprinkle
Finely grated zest of ½ lemon
1½ tbsp sunflower seeds
1½ tbsp clear honey

FOR THE FILLING
700g pink dessert
   gooseberries
40g caster sugar
1½ tbsp cornflour
3 tbsp elderflower cordial

Pink dessert gooseberries have a short season, worth making the most of, as they are much sweeter than green gooseberries and their skins are more tender. That said, if they are not available, this recipe works perfectly well with regular, green gooseberries, but you will need to use more sugar to counteract their sourness and acidity – generally twice the amount. Taste the fruit before using, which will help you to adjust the sugar quantity according to personal preference. You will need a 1-litre shallow pie dish.

1 Put the oats in a small bowl. Pour over the apple juice, mix together and set aside to soak. Roughly chop the hazelnuts and almonds.

2 Sift the flour into a large bowl with the ginger, cinnamon, nutmeg and salt. Cut the butter into 1cm cubes and rub it into the flour with your fingertips until the mixture resembles coarse breadcrumbs. Stir in the demerara sugar, lemon zest and sunflower seeds.

3 Add the soaked oats and chopped nuts to the rubbed-in mixture and drizzle over the honey. Mix everything together using your hands.

4 Wash and then lightly flour your hands. Press the topping together into clumps (about 3–4cm), rather like large pieces of granola. Unevenly shaped, flaky pieces will give a better, crunchier texture to the baked topping than well formed pieces. Place the pieces of topping on a large plate or baking sheet.

5 Heat the oven to 190°C/gas mark 5 and grease the pie dish.

6 Top and tail the gooseberries, then rinse under cold, running water. Place in the pie dish (they should be only 1 or 2 layers deep), sprinkle over the caster sugar and cornflour and stir well. Pour in the elderflower cordial and stir again.

7 Cover the fruit with the pieces of topping, fairly loosely and irregularly, as this will help the heat to circulate around the dish and will crisp the topping nicely during baking. Sprinkle a little demerara sugar over the surface.

8 Bake in the middle of the oven for 15–20 minutes, then lower the oven setting to 180°C/gas mark 4 and continue to cook for a further 10–15 minutes, or until the topping is very crisp, a good golden brown colour and the fruit is hot and bubbling. You may need to cover the dish with foil towards the end of the cooking time, if the topping starts to catch around the edges before the pudding is cooked through. Serve hot or warm.

CHERRY COBBLER

SERVES 6

Butter, to grease
1kg black cherries
2 tbsp cornflour
3 tbsp soft light brown sugar
2 tbsp cherry brandy
    (or another fruit liqueur)

FOR THE TOPPING
40g dried sour cherries
170g self-raising flour,
    plus extra to dust
Pinch of salt
60g unsalted butter
30g demerara sugar
150ml buttermilk
1 tbsp milk
60g flaked almonds

This is a very simple pudding that can be made with just about any type of soft fruit. The topping is essentially a soft scone mixture that spreads a little during cooking, to partially cover the fruit. Try adding chopped nuts and spices to the topping to add a different flavour and texture to the finished pudding. You will need a 1 litre shallow pie dish.

1 Heat the oven to 190°C/gas mark 5. Grease the pie dish with butter.

2 Pit the cherries and put them into a large bowl. Add the cornflour and light brown sugar and stir gently to coat the fruit evenly. Transfer to the pie dish and drizzle over the cherry brandy. Set aside while you make the topping.

3 For the topping, chop the dried cherries roughly and put them in a small bowl. Pour over enough boiling water to cover them completely and leave to stand for 10 minutes.

4 Meanwhile, sift the flour into a large bowl with the salt. Cut the butter into 1cm cubes and rub it into the flour with your fingertips until the mixture resembles coarse breadcrumbs. Stir in the demerara sugar and make a well in the centre.

5 Drain the dried cherries and add them to the well with the buttermilk. Stir briskly using a cutlery knife until the dough starts to come together. Gather it with lightly floured hands; it should be very soft and will feel quite sticky, but not wet.

6 Drop unevenly shaped pieces of the dough, roughly 1 tbsp in size, onto the fruit, without completely covering the fruit, so the steam can escape through the gaps as it cooks. The dough will also rise and spread during baking.

7 Brush the dough with the milk and scatter over the flaked almonds. Bake in the top third of the oven for 25–30 minutes, or until well risen, golden brown and the fruit is hot and bubbling up through the topping. Serve hot or warm.

RASPBERRY AND CINNAMON TORTE

SERVES 8

150g butter, at room
    temperature, plus extra
    to grease
150g self-raising flour
1 tsp ground cinnamon
150g golden caster sugar
150g ground almonds
1 egg

225g raspberries, thawed
    if frozen
Icing sugar and ground
    cinnamon, to dust

TO SERVE
Melba sauce
    (see page 149)

Make this delicious torte when homegrown raspberries are abundant, or use frozen raspberries to bring some summer colour to a drab winter day. It is also very good made with poached apricots or rhubarb in place of the raspberries. You can add some chopped nuts to the cakey-textured base if you like, too. You will need a 22cm round springform cake tin.

1 Heat the oven to 180°C/gas mark 4. Grease the springform tin and line the base with non-stick baking parchment.

2 Sift the flour and cinnamon into a medium bowl. Cut the butter into small chunks and add to the bowl along with the sugar and ground almonds. Break the egg into a separate, small bowl and beat lightly with a fork until broken up. Stir the egg into the rest of the ingredients and beat thoroughly with a wooden spoon or electric beaters until just smooth.

3 Spread half of the mixture into the prepared tin and gently smooth the surface.

4 Sprinkle the raspberries over the mixture and dot the remaining torte mixture in tablespoonfuls on top so that it almost covers the fruit.

5 Stand the tin on a baking sheet and bake in the middle of the oven for 40 minutes, or until the cake feels just firm and slightly springy, loosely covering the top with foil if it is becoming too brown before it has had a chance to cook through.

6 Remove from the oven and leave to cool in the tin for 1 hour, to allow it to set completely.

7 Remove the cooled torte from the tin and dust lightly with icing sugar sifted with a little cinnamon.

8 Serve just warm with the Melba sauce, and some cream or Greek yoghurt on the side if you like.

FRUIT JELLIES

Jellies are a fantastic way of serving fresh fruit and fruit purées, and make a light and elegant end to a meal. Their jewel-like colours and the way they catch the light, especially when served on a bright white plate, can be stunning.

Jellies are served cold, as gelatine will melt as it warms up, causing a beautifully moulded jelly to end up a colourful puddle on the plate. Chill jellies until about 20–30 minutes before they are required, as to serve them straight from the fridge can mean a firm textured jelly on the plate rather than one that is meltingly soft. A jelly made of a very acidic mixture, such as citrus juice, will tend to have a softer set, so can be taken out of the fridge later.

You can experiment with all manner of cups, glasses and dishes as jelly moulds – just pour water into them to wet the inside, and tip the water out before pouring in the jelly mixture. It is a good idea to stick to moulds with reasonably smooth sides to make it easier to unmould the jelly in one piece.

Gelatine is made commercially from animal bone and skin, which sounds unappealing for use in desserts. However, no taste of its origin can be detected in the final flavour of the dish, and those who choose not to use it can substitute vegetarian alternatives such as agar agar. (When using alternatives, follow the packet instructions.) The texture of the finished dish may not be quite as smooth and refined as a dish made with gelatine, but it is a good option for vegetarians.

Gelatine can be purchased in powdered and leaf form. We tend to use powdered when a cold liquid is to be set, and leaf gelatine to set a warm mixture. Powdered gelatine should be soaked (or sponged) in a little cold liquid, then gently warmed to dissolve it. In this liquid form it then combines easily with a cold liquid mixture.

Leaf gelatine is soaked in cold water to soften it, then stirred into a warm mixture to dissolve it, making it ideal for warm mixtures such as a vanilla custard.

TECHNIQUE
USING POWDERED GELATINE

Powdered gelatine needs to be rehydrated with water, a technique called 'sponging'. The gelatine is then dissolved gently over a low heat before use.

1 Sprinkle the powdered gelatine evenly over a minimum of 3 tbsp cold water in a small saucepan.

2 Set aside to 'sponge' (absorb water) for 5–10 minutes. The gelatine will become jelly-like and translucent. The sponged gelatine can happily sit like this for a while.

3 When ready to use, put the saucepan over a very low heat and leave the gelatine to dissolve gently, until no grains are visible. Avoid stirring or splashing up the sides of the pan.

A note on using powdered gelatine...

✱ Don't dissolve gelatine over a high heat. If gelatine gets too hot, it can lose some of its setting properties. Once the powdered gelatine is fully dissolved and has the appearance of a clear, smooth liquid, it is ready to use. Make sure the liquid or mixture you are adding dissolved gelatine to is not fridge cold, or the gelatine will cool very quickly into strings and lumps as it is added, resulting in an uneven set and unsatisfactory texture.

USING LEAF GELATINE

Leaf gelatine is much easier to use than powdered, but because it needs a warm to hot liquid or mixture to dissolve, it can't be used universally, as powdered gelatine can.

1 Place the leaf gelatine in a bowl of cold water, ensuring the leaves are covered and leave for 5–10 minutes to soften.

3 Give the sheets a squeeze to remove excess water, then add them to a warm to hot liquid or mixture, to dissolve them completely. Strain the mixture, if possible, to ensure all the gelatine is completely dissolved, checking the sieve for any undissolved gelatine.

A note on using leaf gelatine...

✽ You need to be aware that different brands of commercial leaf gelatine vary in strength. The gelatine recipes in this book have been tested with bronze leaf gelatine. If you are using a different variety, follow the recommended quantity on the packet per 570–600ml liquid.

Don't use warm or hot water to sponge leaf gelatine, or it will melt and dissolve in the water, leaving nothing to lift out.

2 Once the leaf gelatine is soft to the touch, pick out the individual leaves. Count the sheets in and out to ensure they are all removed and used (as the leaf gelatine absorbs water it turns translucent and is difficult to see in the water).

ORANGE AND PASSION FRUIT JELLY

SERVES 4	

3 tbsp water
3½ tsp powdered gelatine
10–12 ripe passion fruit (or
    200ml passion fruit juice)
2–3 tbsp caster sugar,
    to taste

400ml orange juice (from
    about 4–5 large oranges)

TO SERVE
2 oranges
2 passion fruit

This recipe can be adapted to use any sweetened fruit juice, except pineapple which won't set well with gelatine. Just taste it first to ensure it is sweet enough as dishes tend to need to be a little sweeter when being served chilled. You will need a 600–650ml jelly mould or 4 dariole moulds.

1 Put the water into a small saucepan, sprinkle over the gelatine and leave for 5 minutes to absorb the water and become spongy (see page 36). Place over the lowest heat and leave to dissolve, without stirring.

2 Halve the passion fruit, scoop out the seeds and juice into a sieve over a bowl and press with the back of a wooden spoon to extract the juice. In a second pan over a low heat, dissolve the sugar in half of the orange juice, stirring.

3 Pour the warm orange juice into the melted gelatine and stir well. Stir in the passion fruit juice and remaining orange juice. Taste and add sugar if necessary.

4 Rinse out a jelly mould or 4 dariole moulds with cold water, and pour in the mixture. Refrigerate for at least 4 hours, or until the jellies are completely set.

5 Half an hour before serving, take the jellies out of the fridge. Segment the oranges (see page 10) and scoop out the pulp from the passion fruit; mix together. To turn out the jellies, loosen the top with a finger. Dip each mould into a dish of boiling water (just to the rim), then invert over a damp serving plate. Give the mould a sharp sideways shake side to release the jelly onto the plate. Serve with the oranges and passion fruit.

Variations

✱ Use good quality fruit juice (from a carton), such as raspberry and pomegranate.

PINK GRAPEFRUIT AND CHAMPAGNE JELLY

SERVES 6–8	
3 pink grapefruit	150g caster sugar, or more
550ml Champagne	to taste
20ml ginger wine	5 sheets of leaf gelatine

This is a beautiful, clear jelly that is shown off to its best served in individual glasses or ramekins.

1 Place 6–8 medium ramekins or glasses in the fridge to cool. Segment the grapefruit (see page 10).

2 Put the Champagne, ginger wine and 150g caster sugar in a medium saucepan and gently heat until the sugar has dissolved. Taste and add more sugar if desired.

3 Meanwhile, place the gelatine sheets in a bowl of cold water and leave to soak for at least 5 minutes, until softened (see page 38).

4 Squeeze the excess water from the softened gelatine leaves and drop them into the warmed Champagne liquor. Stir to dissolve the gelatine, checking that it has dissolved fully; the liquid should be clear. Pour the liquid into a jug.

5 Pour a little liquid into the bottom of the chilled ramekins or glasses and chill them for about 30 minutes, or until almost set.

6 Remove the jellies from the fridge, divide the grapefruit segments between them, then pour on enough jelly mixture to nearly cover the segments, but holding back enough for a further layer.

7 Return the jellies to the fridge until nearly set again; this may take an hour. Keep the jug with the remaining mixture warm to prevent the jelly mixture setting (stand it in a bowl of warm water if the kitchen is cool).

8 Remove the jellies from the fridge and pour on a final layer of jelly, ensuring the grapefruit is completely covered, then chill until set. Remove the jellies from the fridge 20 minutes before serving, to allow them to soften a little.

RHUBARB AND CUSTARD JELLIES

SERVES 8–10

1kg rhubarb, ideally pink,
   thin-stemmed
1 orange
225g golden caster sugar
About 6 sheets of leaf
   gelatine
Pink food colouring,
   preferably paste (optional)

FOR THE CUSTARD
300ml whole milk
300ml double cream
1 vanilla pod
4 egg yolks
125g caster sugar
About 5 sheets of leaf
   gelatine

If you make these jellies with early, forced, pale pink rhubarb, they will have a lovely natural pink colour. If using outdoor rhubarb, you can cheat and add a very little food colouring. Serve with shortbread biscuits.

1 Wash and trim the rhubarb, then cut into short lengths. Juice the orange. Place the rhubarb, sugar and orange juice in a saucepan. Cover and simmer for 3–5 minutes, or until the rhubarb is just soft. Remove about 1 tbsp rhubarb per person for decoration, and set aside to cool. Continue to cook the remaining rhubarb for a further 3–5 minutes, or until very soft.

2 Remove from the heat and strain through a fine sieve (lined with a muslin cloth if you have one, for the clearest of jellies), pushing gently with the back of a wooden spoon to make sure all the juice is released. Once strained, discard the rhubarb left in the sieve and measure the liquid. Calculate the amount of gelatine leaves required to set the rhubarb juice according to the packet instructions. Place the gelatine leaves in a bowl of cold water and leave to soak for 5 minutes (see page 38).

3 Return the rhubarb juice to a pan and warm over a low heat. If it isn't very pink, add a drop or two of pink food colouring to achieve the desired colour. Once hot, remove the pan from the heat, squeeze the excess water from the soaked gelatine leaves and add them to the rhubarb liquid. Stir until the gelatine has completely dissolved, then leave the jelly in the warm pan and allow it to cool to tepid while you prepare the custard layer.

4 Pour the milk and cream into a saucepan. Cut the vanilla pod in half lengthways and scrape out the seeds. Add the pod and seeds to the pan and place over a medium heat. Scald the mixture, by gently heating it until steaming, and bubbles appear around the edge of the pan. Take off the heat and remove the vanilla pod and any skin that has formed.

5 Put the egg yolks and sugar in a medium bowl and stir to combine. Pour in a little of the scalded milk mixture and stir, then add the remaining milk gradually, stirring continuously until fully combined. Rinse out the saucepan.

6 Return the mixture to the cleaned pan. Place over a low to medium heat and stir continuously with a wooden spoon until thickened. To check that the custard has thickened enough, remove from the heat and draw the back of the spoon through the liquid. It should coat the back of the spoon evenly and not drop away and pool at the base of the spoon, and when you draw a clean finger down the back of the spoon through the custard, the trail should remain. When you reach this point immediately strain the custard through a fine sieve into a bowl.

7 Measure the custard and calculate three quarters of the amount of gelatine recommended on the packet instructions. Soak the gelatine leaves in a bowl of cold water for 5 minutes, then remove from the water, squeeze out any excess liquid and add them to the warm custard. Stir well until dissolved. Divide the custard equally between 8–10 serving glasses and transfer to the fridge to cool and set.

8 When the custard has just set, divide the rhubarb jelly between the glasses and return the dishes to the fridge to set.

9 Take the jellies out of the fridge 20 minutes before serving. Top with a little of the reserved poached rhubarb and serve.

2

STEAMED PUDDINGS, SOUFFLÉS AND CRÊPES

These puddings all use the transforming power of eggs.
Steamed puddings – typically made with a creamed cake
mixture – are the ultimate comfort food, perfect for a cold
winter's day. Soufflés use the amazing ability of whisked egg
white to trap air in order to achieve their wonderful high rise.
Always impressive and easier to make than they appear to be,
hot soufflés are sophisticated enough for a special meal.
Crêpes are made from a light batter, enriched with eggs. One
of the most versatile and speediest of puddings, they are an
easy way to round off a simple family meal.

STEAMED PUDDINGS

The method for making a delicious steamed pudding is the same as that for the most basic of sponge cakes. The mixture is then cooked slowly in moist, steamy heat and, when made well, will have a lightness that will certainly surprise those who suffered heavy school steamed puddings.

Steamed puddings can be prepared well before you sit down to eat, gently steaming until you are ready to serve: a stress-free but indulgent end to the meal. Just remember to top up the water in the pan occasionally so it doesn't boil dry.

You don't need any special equipment to steam a pudding; we use a large pan with a lid, a piece of egg box to keep the pudding basin off the base of the pan, and greaseproof paper, foil and string as a lid to cover the pudding basin.

To test if a steamed pudding is cooked, insert a skewer into the middle, through the foil and paper cover. As you remove the skewer, check that there is no raw mixture clinging to it, only crumbs. If it is not ready, cover the hole in the cover with a sticky label and continue to steam the pudding until cooked.

TECHNIQUE

PREPARING A PUDDING FOR STEAMING

1 Put a trivet into a large saucepan (big enough to easily hold the pudding basin) that has a tight-fitting lid. Alternatively, use a folded piece of thick cardboard or a cardboard egg carton (trimmed to fit). This will keep the base of the pudding basin off the bottom of the saucepan, which is its hottest part.

2 Cut out one sheet of foil and 2 sheets of greaseproof paper, at least twice the diameter of the top of the pudding basin. Make a small pleat, about 3cm wide, in the middle of the foil.

3 Put one sheet of greaseproof paper on top of the other and make a similar pleat. Lightly butter one side of the double greaseproof paper. Cut a piece of string, the length of your open arms.

4 Spoon the mixture into the pudding basin and level it out. Place the greaseproof paper buttered side down on top of the pudding basin.

5 Cover with the sheet of foil and push it down and around the top rim of the pudding basin.

6 Fold the string in half and place the doubled string around the pudding basin under the lip, over the foil. Feed the cut ends between the folded end and tighten the string. Separate the 2 cut ends and bring each string around the pudding basin, still under the lip, then tie tightly in a knot.

7 Hold the 2 strings together, take them over the pudding basin to the other side and tuck them through the string on the other side, leaving the ends loose to create a handle for lifting the pudding. Tie the string securely.

8 Lift up the foil around the string to expose the greaseproof paper and trim the paper fairly close to the string. Trim the foil to leave a 3–4cm border.

9 Tuck the foil around the greaseproof paper towards the lip of the pudding basin, ensuring all the greaseproof paper is enclosed in the foil. Your pudding is now ready for steaming.

1 A makeshift trivet in place (to keep the base of the basin off the bottom of the saucepan).

2 Pleating the foil that will cover the pudding.

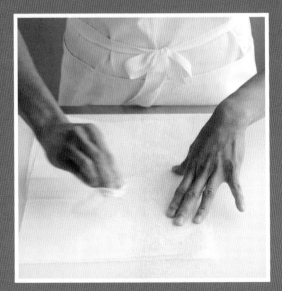

3 Buttering the doubled greaseproof paper.

4 Covering the pudding with the buttered greaseproof paper.

(Continued overleaf)

5 Covering the top of the pudding basin with the sheet of foil.

6 Tying the string under the rim of the basin to hold the foil cover firmly in place.

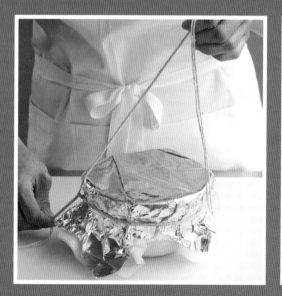

7 Creating a handle from the excess string to make it easier to lift the pudding from the pan.

8 Trimming away the excess greaseproof paper, before tucking the foil border up over the paper (shown right).

TREACLE SPONGE

SERVES 4–6

120g butter, softened,
  plus extra to grease
75g golden syrup
3 tsp fresh white
  breadcrumbs
120g caster sugar

1 lemon
2 large eggs, at room
  temperature
120g self-raising flour
1 tsp ground ginger

This all-time traditional favourite is best served with crème anglaise (see page 146) or thick vanilla custard (see page 148). You will need an 850ml pudding basin.

1 Grease the pudding basin well with butter. Prepare the saucepan for steaming and the cover for the pudding (see page 48). Weigh the golden syrup into the bowl and sprinkle over the breadcrumbs.

2 Cream the butter and sugar in a large bowl until pale and fluffy. Finely grate the zest from half of the lemon and stir into the mixture.

3 Beat the eggs lightly in a separate bowl to loosen and gradually add to the creamed butter and sugar, beating well after each addition.

4 Sift the flour and ginger together and carefully fold into the mixture with a large metal spoon.

5 Spoon the mixture into the pudding basin and level the surface. Cover with the greaseproof paper and foil and secure under the rim (see page 48).

6 Place the pudding basin on the trivet in the steamer and pour in enough boiling water to come at least halfway up the sides of the basin (not touching the foil). Place the pan over a medium heat and ensure the water is bubbling gently, but still not coming into contact with the foil. Put the lid on the saucepan and steam the pudding for 1¼–1½ hours, checking the water level in the saucepan frequently and topping up with hot water to ensure it doesn't burn dry and no heat is lost.

7 Lift the pudding out of the steamer and remove the string, foil and greaseproof paper. Wearing oven gloves, invert a serving dish over the bowl and turn both over together. Give the pudding basin a sharp shake, which should release the pudding, then carefully remove the basin.

Variations

✳ **Individual sponges** Butter 6 individual pudding basins or dariole moulds and put 1 tbsp golden syrup and 1 tsp breadcrumbs in the bottom of each. Divide the mixture between them and proceed as for the main recipe, covering them individually with foil and greaseproof paper. (As this is time-consuming, you might prefer to use heatproof plastic pudding basins with snap-on lids.) Reduce the cooking time to 25 minutes.

✳ **Lemon sponge pudding** Omit the syrup, breadcrumbs and ground ginger. Add the finely grated zest of 2 lemons to the mixture and proceed as for the main recipe, cooking the pudding for 1½ hours. Warm 150g lemon curd to a thick coating consistency and pour over the pudding before serving.

MEDJOOL DATE AND CARDAMOM PUDDING

SERVES 4–6	
120g butter, softened, plus extra to grease	120g soft dark brown sugar
35g date syrup	1 lemon
40g golden syrup	2 large eggs, at room temperature
3 tsp fresh white breadcrumbs	8 Medjool dates
3 cardamom pods, or ½ tsp ground cardamom	120g self-raising flour

You will need an 850ml pudding basin.

1 Grease the pudding basin well with butter. Prepare the saucepan for steaming and the cover for the pudding (see page 48). Combine the 2 syrups in the bottom of the basin and sprinkle over the breadcrumbs.

2 Crack open the cardamom pods and extract the seeds, then grind the seeds to a powder, using a pestle and mortar.

3 Cream the butter and sugar in a large bowl until pale and fluffy. Finely grate the zest from half of the lemon and stir into the mixture.

4 Beat the eggs lightly in a separate bowl to loosen and gradually add to the creamed butter and sugar, beating well after each addition.

5 Remove the stones from the dates, then coarsely chop them and stir into the mixture.

6 Sift the flour and cardamom together and carefully fold into the mixture with a large metal spoon.

7 Spoon the mixture into the pudding basin and level the surface. Cover with the greaseproof paper and foil and secure under the rim (see page 48).

8 Place the pudding basin on the trivet in the steamer and pour in enough boiling water to come at least halfway up the sides of the basin (not touching the foil). Place the pan over a medium heat and ensure the water is bubbling gently, but still not coming into contact with the foil. Put the lid on the pan and steam the pudding for 2–2¼ hours, checking the water level in the saucepan frequently and topping up with hot water to ensure it doesn't burn dry and no heat is lost.

9 Lift the pudding out of the steamer and remove the string, foil and greaseproof paper. Wearing oven gloves, invert a serving dish over the bowl and turn both over together. Give the pudding basin a sharp shake, which should release the pudding, then carefully remove the basin. Serve with Greek yoghurt, sweetened with a little runny honey.

Variation

✳ **Individual sponges** Butter 6 individual pudding basins or dariole moulds and put 1 tbsp mixed date syrup and golden syrup and 1 tsp breadcrumbs in the bottom of each. Divide the mixture between them and proceed as for the main recipe, covering them individually with foil and greaseproof paper. (As this is time-consuming, you might prefer to use heatproof plastic pudding basins with snap-on lids.) Reduce the cooking time to 30 minutes.

CHRISTMAS PUDDING

60g mixed dried apricots
and dried figs
1 lemon
50g raisins
30g currants
50g sultanas
20g chopped mixed peel
75ml brown ale
½ tbsp rum
1 teabag
30g pitted prunes
60g butter, softened, plus
extra to grease
½ small dessert apple

20g blanched almonds
85g soft dark brown sugar
½ tbsp treacle
1 small egg, at room
temperature
30g self-raising flour
¼ tsp ground mixed spice
Pinch of ground cinnamon
Small pinch of freshly
grated nutmeg
Small pinch of ground ginger
Small pinch of salt
60g fresh white breadcrumbs

The dried fruit needs to be soaked overnight, ahead of steaming. You will need a 1 litre pudding basin.

1 Roughly chop the apricots and figs. Finely grate the zest from the lemon, then squeeze the juice from half the lemon. Put the raisins, currants, sultanas and peel into a bowl and add the ale, rum and lemon zest and juice. Make a pot of tea using the teabag and let cool. Put the prunes in a separate bowl and pour over the cold tea. Cover both bowls and leave to soak overnight.

2 When ready to steam the pudding, grease the pudding basin with butter. Prepare the saucepan for steaming and the cover for the pudding (see page 48).

3 Drain the prunes, discarding the tea, then coarsely chop them and add to the fruit and beer. Grate the unpeeled apple and finely chop the almonds.

4 Beat the butter and sugar together in a large bowl until pale and fluffy. Stir in the treacle.

5 Beat the egg and gradually add to the creamed mixture, beating well after each addition.

6 Sift the flour, spices and salt together over the mixture. Add the breadcrumbs and fold in with a large spoon. Stir in the nuts, dried fruit and soaking liquor.

7 Spoon the mixture into the pudding basin and level the surface. Lay the greaseproof paper and foil cover on top and secure under the rim, leaving a string handle (see page 48).

8 Place the pudding basin on the trivet in the steamer and pour in enough boiling water to come at least halfway up the sides of the basin (not touching the foil). Place the pan over a medium heat and ensure the water is maintaining a steady boil.

9 Put the lid on the pan and steam the pudding for 8 hours, checking the water level in the saucepan frequently and topping up with hot water to ensure it doesn't burn dry.

10 After 8 hours, lift the pudding carefully out of the steamer and remove the cover. Wearing oven gloves, invert a serving dish over the bowl and turn both over together. Give the basin a sharp shake, which should release the pudding onto the dish. Serve the Christmas pudding with brandy butter or custard.

A note on reheating...

✱ Once the pudding is cooked it can be cooled intact, with the foil still on, and kept in a cool place for a few months. To reheat the pudding, steam it as above for 2–2½ hours.

SOUFFLÉS

Timing is undeniably important with a hot soufflé, but the actual preparation is not as tricky as you might imagine, and much of the cooking can be done in advance. In fact, once the hot soufflé mixture has been put into the ramekins, they can even be frozen and baked from frozen the following day, adding about an extra 4 minutes to the cooking time. It is a good idea to make an extra soufflé and test the cooking time before the guests arrive, as the thickness and size of the dish can slightly alter the cooking time.

When making a soufflé, the trick is to make sure that the base mixture ('panade') is soft enough to allow you to fold in the whisked egg whites without knocking out all the air bubbles, and that the egg whites are whisked stiffly enough to trap sufficient air. The trapped air bubbles expand in the oven, raising the soufflé as they do so. Prepare the ramekins carefully so the mixture can rise up the sides without getting stuck.

The perfect soufflé will rise up above the top of the ramekin, have a straight top and have a generous teaspoonful of soft, undercooked mixture in the middle, which acts rather like a sauce for the rest of the soufflé. You can also provide a jug of raspberry (or other fruit) coulis or cream for guests to pour into the centre of their soufflé once they've taken their first spoonful.

Baking a large soufflé

✱ The recipes in this section are for individual soufflés, but if you would rather make a large soufflé to share, use a 15cm soufflé dish and increase the cooking time to 25–30 minutes.

A note on the crème pâtissière...

✱ Avoid the crème pâtissière cooling completely before folding through the egg whites, or it will stiffen too much. If this does happen, warm the crème pâtissière over a low heat to soften.

A note on stabilising egg whites...

✱ In recipes where caster sugar is added to whisked egg whites, whisking a spoonful of the measured sugar into the whites once they've reached their desired peak will stabilise them. The mix is whisked until stiff again (about 30 seconds with an electric whisk). The whites will then hold for longer before collapsing.

TECHNIQUE
SEPARATING EGGS

To separate an egg, crack the egg on the edge of a table or use a cutlery knife. Avoid too much pressure or you will break the egg in half. You only want to crack the shell.

Carefully ease apart the shell halves over a medium to large bowl. Some white will fall into the bowl; it is important that none of the yolk does.

Carefully pass the egg yolk between the 2 half shells, without breaking it, allowing the white to fall into the bowl as you do so.

Once all (or most) of the white is in the bowl, all that may be left on the yolk is the 'chalaza', or thread. Carefully prise away from the yolk, with the edge of a shell, so it falls into the bowl. Put the yolk in another small bowl.

SEVILLE ORANGE SOUFFLÉ

SERVES 4–6

10g unsalted butter, to grease
50g caster sugar, plus
   1–2 tbsp to coat the
   ramekins
300ml whole milk
1 vanilla pod

1–2 Seville oranges
3 eggs
15g plain flour
15g cornflour
2–3 tbsp icing sugar

You will need 4–6 ramekins, or a 15cm soufflé dish to make one large soufflé (see left).

1 Heat the oven to 200°C/gas mark 6 and put a baking tray in to heat. (The hot baking tray will provide 'bottom heat', giving the soufflés an immediate burst of heat from the base to encourage a quick and even rise.)

2 Melt the butter and use to brush 4–6 ramekin dishes, then pour the 1–2 tbsp caster sugar into the first ramekin. Tilt the ramekin to coat the bottom and sides evenly with the sugar, then pour the excess into the next ramekin. Repeat until all the ramekins are coated in sugar.

3 To make the crème pâtissière, put the milk into a medium saucepan and bring to scalding point (see page 155) over a medium heat. Meanwhile, split the vanilla pod lengthways and scrape out the seeds. Finely grate the zest from the orange(s) and squeeze the juice from 1 orange. Add the vanilla pod and seeds, and the grated orange zest to the milk to infuse.

4 Separate the eggs (see left), putting the whites into a large bowl and the yolks into a separate, medium bowl.

5 When the milk is scalding hot, take off the heat, skim off any skin that may have formed and remove the vanilla pod. Mix the egg yolks with all but 1 tbsp of the 50g caster sugar, add a splash of the milk, then both flours, and combine well to ensure there are no lumps. Add the remaining milk and stir. Rinse out the milk pan to remove the milk solids.

6 Return the mixture to the rinsed out pan and place over a low to medium heat. Bring to the boil, stirring continuously

with a wooden spoon. It will go lumpy, but stir vigorously and it will become smooth. Lower the heat and simmer for 2 minutes. Remove from the heat, transfer to a bowl and leave to cool slightly, then stir in the orange juice. Taste and adjust the sweetness with a little more caster sugar if necessary.

7 Whisk the egg whites to medium-stiff peaks (see page 109), then whisk in the remaining 1 tbsp caster sugar, to stabilise. Take a large spoonful of the whites and fold it into the crème pâtissière, to loosen it, then gently fold in the remaining whites.

8 Fill the prepared ramekins with the soufflé mixture and use a palette knife to level the tops, scraping away any excess mixture. Clean the outside of the ramekin if necessary and 'top hat' the soufflé by running the tip of a cutlery knife around the top inner rim of the ramekin, which will help to create an even rise.

9 Place the ramekins on the hot baking sheet in the top third of the oven and bake for 8–12 minutes until cooked but still uniformly wobbly when shaken.

10 Remove the soufflés from the oven, sift the icing sugar over the tops through a fine sieve and serve immediately. There should be about 1 tsp undercooked soufflé mixture in the centre of each.

Variation

✱ If Seville oranges are not in season, stir in 2–3 tbsp good quality Seville orange marmalade (ideally thin-cut) instead.

VANILLA SOUFFLÉ

SERVES 4–6

10g unsalted butter, to grease
50g caster sugar, plus
   1–2 tbsp to coat the
   ramekins
300ml whole milk
1 vanilla pod

3 eggs
15g plain flour
15g cornflour
2–3 tbsp icing sugar

You will need 4–6 ramekins, or a 15cm soufflé dish to make one large soufflé (see page 56).

1 Heat the oven to 200°C/gas mark 6 and put a baking tray in to heat. (The hot baking tray will provide 'bottom heat', giving the soufflés an immediate burst of heat from the base to encourage a quick and even rise.)

2 Melt the butter and use to brush 4–6 ramekin dishes, then pour the 1–2 tbsp caster sugar into the first ramekin. Tilt the ramekin to coat the bottom and sides evenly with the sugar, then pour the excess into the next ramekin. Repeat until all the ramekins are coated in sugar.

3 To make the crème pâtissière, put the milk into a medium saucepan and bring to scalding point (see page 155) over a medium heat. Split the vanilla pod lengthways and scrape out the seeds. Add the pod and seeds to the milk to infuse.

4 Separate the eggs (see page 56), putting the whites into a large bowl and the yolks into a separate, medium bowl.

5 When the milk is scalding hot, take off the heat, skim off any skin that may have formed and remove the vanilla pod. Mix the egg yolks with all but 1 tbsp of the 50g caster sugar, add a splash of the milk, then both flours, and combine well to ensure there are no lumps. Add the remaining milk and stir. Rinse out the milk pan to remove the milk solids.

6 Return the mixture to the rinsed out pan and place over a low to medium heat. Bring to the boil, stirring continuously with a wooden spoon. It will go lumpy, but stir vigorously and it will become smooth. Lower the heat and simmer for 2 minutes. Transfer to a bowl and leave to cool slightly.

7 Whisk the egg whites to medium-stiff peaks (see page 109), then whisk in the remaining 1 tbsp caster sugar, to stabilise.

Take a large spoonful of the whites and fold it into the crème pâtissière, to loosen it, then gently fold in the remaining whites.

8 Fill the prepared ramekins with the soufflé mixture and use a palette knife to level the tops, scraping away any excess mixture. Clean the outside of the ramekin if necessary and 'top hat' the soufflé by running the tip of a cutlery knife around the top inner rim of the ramekin, to facilitate an even rise.

9 Place the ramekins on the hot baking sheet in the top third of the oven and bake for 8–12 minutes until cooked but still uniformly wobbly when shaken.

10 Remove the soufflés from the oven, sift the icing sugar over the tops through a fine sieve and serve immediately. There should be about 1 tsp undercooked soufflé mixture in the centre of each.

Variations

✴ **Raspberry soufflé** Omit the vanilla pod. Add 100ml raspberry purée (about 200g frozen, defrosted, sieved raspberries) to the crème pâtissière. Taste and adjust the sweetness by adding up to 1 tbsp more sugar, then proceed as above.

✴ **Prune and Armagnac soufflé** Gently simmer 75g prunes in 75ml Armagnac and 75ml water until soft and at least one third of the liquid has evaporated. Leave to cool, then purée to a smooth paste. Proceed as for the main recipe, using a few drops of vanilla extract instead of the vanilla pod in the thickened crème pâtissière. Spoon 1 tsp of the prune purée into the prepared ramekins, then stir the remainder into the crème pâtissière and proceed as for the main recipe.

HAZELNUT NOUGATINE SOUFFLÉ

SERVES 4–6	
FOR THE NOUGATINE	**FOR THE SOUFFLÉ**
Oil, to grease	10g unsalted butter, to grease
50g skinned hazelnuts	3 eggs
75g caster sugar	300ml whole milk
½ tsp glucose syrup	50g caster sugar
	15g plain flour
	15g cornflour
	2–3 tbsp icing sugar

You will need 4–6 ramekins, or a 15cm soufflé dish to make one large soufflé (see page 56).

1 For the nougatine, heat the oven to 180°C/gas mark 4 and very lightly oil a baking sheet. Finely chop the hazelnuts, place on a second baking sheet and toast in the oven until pale golden; keep warm. Put the sugar and glucose syrup in a heavy-based frying pan and set over a low heat. As the sugar begins to take on colour, use a fork to gently encourage the unmelted sugar to the edges of the pan and achieve an even colouring. When all the sugar is caramelised, add the warm nuts and turn to coat in the caramel.

2 Immediately tip the nougatine mixture onto the oiled baking sheet and allow to cool completely, then break the nougatine into pieces and grind in a food processor to a fine powder.

3 For the soufflé, heat the oven to 200°C/gas mark 6 and put a baking tray in to heat. (The hot baking tray will provide 'bottom heat', giving the soufflés an immediate burst of heat from the base to encourage a quick and even rise.)

4 Melt the butter and use to brush 4–6 ramekin dishes, then tip 2 tbsp of the ground nougatine into the first ramekin. Tilt the ramekin to coat the bottom and sides evenly, then pour the excess into the next ramekin. Repeat to coat all the ramekins.

5 Separate the eggs (see page 56), putting the whites into a large bowl and the yolks into a separate, medium bowl.

6 To make the crème pâtissière, put the milk into a medium saucepan and bring to scalding point (see page 155) over a medium heat.

When the milk is scalding hot, take the pan off the heat and skim off any skin that may have formed. Mix the egg yolks with all but 1 tbsp of the 50g caster sugar, add a splash of the milk, then both flours, and combine well to ensure there are no lumps. Add the remaining milk and stir. Rinse out the milk pan to remove the milk solids.

7 Return the mixture to the rinsed out pan and place over a low to medium heat. Bring to the boil, stirring continuously with a wooden spoon. It will go lumpy, but stir vigorously and it will become smooth. Lower the heat and simmer for 2 minutes. Transfer to a bowl and leave to cool slightly, then stir in the remaining powdered nougatine.

8 Whisk the egg whites to medium-stiff peaks (see page 109), then whisk in the remaining 1 tbsp caster sugar, to stabilise. Take a large spoonful of the whites and fold it into the crème pâtissière, to loosen it, then gently fold in the remaining whites.

9 Fill the prepared ramekins with the soufflé mixture and use a palette knife to level the tops, scraping away any excess mixture. Clean the outside of the ramekin if necessary and 'top hat' the soufflé by running the tip of a cutlery knife around the top inner rim of the ramekin, which will help to create an even rise.

10 Place the ramekins on the hot baking sheet in the top third of the oven and bake for 8–12 minutes until cooked but still uniformly wobbly when shaken.

11 Remove the soufflés from the oven, sift the icing sugar over the tops using a fine sieve and serve immediately. There should be about 1 tsp undercooked soufflé mix in the centre of each.

QUICK CHOCOLATE AND CHERRY SOUFFLÉ

SERVES 4–6

10g unsalted butter
90g caster sugar, plus
   1–2 tbsp to coat the
   ramekins
150g good quality dark
   chocolate, about
   60% cocoa solids
60ml water

½ tsp instant espresso
   powder
3 eggs
1 tbsp Kirsch
100g good quality cherry
   compote, such as Bonne
   Maman
1½ tsp icing sugar

This is a simple soufflé as it doesn't require a crème pâtissière base and uses a bought cherry compote, so a great storecupboard pudding to have at your fingertips. Of course you could use any good quality compote in place of the cherry, or a homemade one if you have time. You will need 4–6 ramekins, or a 15cm soufflé dish to make one large soufflé (see page 56).

1 Heat the oven to 200°C/gas mark 6. Move an oven shelf to the top third of the oven and put a baking sheet on it to heat.

2 Melt the butter and use it to brush 4–6 ramekin dishes, then pour the 1–2 tbsp caster sugar into the first ramekin. Tilt the ramekin to coat the bottom and sides evenly with the sugar, then pour the excess into the next ramekin. Repeat until all the ramekins are coated in sugar.

3 Break the chocolate into small chunks and put into a small saucepan with the water and espresso powder. Melt over a low heat, stirring gently to combine, then remove from the heat and set aside to cool slightly.

4 Separate the eggs (see page 56) into 2 medium bowls. Add all but 1 tbsp of the sugar, and the Kirsch, to the yolks. Using a hand-held electric whisk, whisk this mixture until pale and mousse-like.

5 Using clean beaters, whisk the whites to medium-stiff peaks, (see page 109), then whisk in the reserved 1 tbsp sugar quickly, to stabilise the whites.

6 Stir the melted chocolate mixture into the yolk mixture, just until the mixture is marbled. Stir in one large spoonful of the egg whites to loosen the mixture, then add the remaining whites and carefully fold them in.

7 Divide the cherry compote between the prepared ramekins, then top with the soufflé mixture and use a palette knife to level the tops, scraping away any excess mixture. Clean the outside of the ramekins if necessary.

8 Place the ramekins on the hot baking sheet in the oven and bake for 8–12 minutes, or until cooked but still uniformly wobbly when shaken.

9 Remove the soufflés from the oven, sift the icing sugar over the tops and serve immediately. There should be a generous 1 tsp undercooked soufflé mixture in the centre of each.

CHOCOLATE FONDANTS

SERVES 4 (makes one extra as a test)

FOR THE MOULDS
20g unsalted butter,
    to grease
Cocoa powder, to dust

FOR THE FONDANTS
100g butter
200g good quality dark
    chocolate, about 70%
    cocoa solids
3 eggs, plus 2 extra yolks
100g caster sugar
50g plain flour

Like soufflés, chocolate fondants can be prepared in advance but will need a little extra time to cook if the mixture is fridge cold when it goes into the oven. Making one extra for testing purposes (a treat for the cook) can take the pressure off deciding exactly when to remove the fondants from the oven. They can be prepared up to 24 hours ahead and kept in the fridge until ready to cook. They are delicious served with vanilla ice cream, as the molten centre of the pudding acts as a hot chocolate sauce. You will need 5 dariole moulds, 150ml capacity.

1 Melt the 20g butter and use to brush the insides of 5 dariole moulds. Sift some cocoa powder into each and shake it around so the insides of the moulds are lightly dusted. Tap out any excess and place the moulds in the freezer.

2 Cut the butter into cubes and break the chocolate into pieces. Put the butter and chocolate into a medium heatproof bowl. Bring a pan of water to the boil, then take it off the heat. Stand the bowl over the pan, making sure the base of the bowl is not touching the water. Leave to melt, stirring occasionally.

3 Put the eggs, extra yolks and sugar in a large bowl and whisk using a hand-held electric whisk until thick and mousse-like. This can be done over a steaming pan to speed up the process, but must then be whisked off the heat until cool again.

4 Using a large metal spoon, fold the melted chocolate mix into the egg mixture, then sift and carefully fold in the flour. Divide between the chilled moulds, filling them to 1cm from the top. Refrigerate for at least 30 minutes, or up to 24 hours.

5 Heat the oven to 200°C/gas mark 6.

6 Place the fondants on a baking tray and cook in the oven for 12–15 minutes, depending on the oven (an electric oven will be quicker than a gas oven). Remove the spare 'tester' fondant after 12 minutes to test. It should be well risen and set on the outside but still molten in the centre when you cut into it.

7 When they are ready, take the remaining puddings out of the oven. Leave them to stand for a minute or two, then remove the fondants from the moulds, inverting them onto plates. Serve immediately.

CRÊPES

MAKES about 12

100g plain flour
Pinch of salt
1 egg, plus 1 extra yolk
300ml milk

1 tbsp sunflower or
   light olive oil
30g unsalted butter, for frying

1 Sift the flour and salt into a mixing bowl. Make a well in the centre. Beat the egg and extra yolk in a small bowl with a fork and add them to the well.

2 Stir the eggs, concentrating your stirring only in the eggs, gradually drawing in flour from around the edge. Don't force the flour in, it will be incorporated automatically as you stir the eggs.

3 As the egg mixture becomes thicker, add a little milk to loosen it, then keep stirring. Continue like this until all the flour has been incorporated. Beat to ensure the thick mixture is smooth, then add the remaining milk and oil. Chill the batter in the fridge for at least 30 minutes, which allows the starch cells in the flour to swell (so lightening the batter).

4 When ready to use, check the consistency of the batter; it should be a thin cream consistency. Pour it into a jug.

5 Melt the butter and set aside in a small bowl. Place a small non-stick frying pan (about 16cm diameter) over a low to medium heat. Wipe out the pan with kitchen paper dipped in the melted butter.

6 Pour a little of the batter into the frying pan, just enough to thinly coat the bottom of the pan, about 1–2mm thick. As you pour the batter in, swirl the pan to encourage the batter to cover the bottom completely, then pour off any excess, back into the jug. Return the pan to the heat and use a palette knife to trim away any batter left up the side of the pan from pouring excess batter back into the jug.

7 After 1–2 minutes, use the palette knife to release and lift the edge of the crêpe to check the colour on the underside.

8 When golden brown, use the palette knife and your fingertips to turn the crêpe over. Cook the second side until golden, 1–2 minutes, then carefully remove it from the pan to a plate.

9 As the pancakes are cooked, stack them interleaved with strips of greaseproof paper (about 3cm wide). This will help to keep the crêpes separate as they are piled up. Repeat with the remaining batter, wiping out the pan with kitchen paper dipped in the melted butter for each crêpe.

A note on cooking crêpes...

✱ Often the first couple of crêpes will either be too thick, or thin and will break. Check the consistency of the batter and add a little milk if it is too thick. As you become more familiar with pouring the batter into the pan and swirling it, the crêpes will improve.

✱ Avoid overcooking the crêpes or they will toughen; they need only 1–2 minutes each side. They should be very thin, with no crisp edges. Adjust the heat a little if necessary.

A note on serving crêpes...

✱ Crêpes can be kept warm wrapped in a clean tea towel until they are all cooked and ready to serve.

✱ Crêpes can be kept in the fridge for 1 or 2 days or frozen in a stack, wrapped in foil and defrosted before use. To warm them through, place the wrapped crêpes in a low oven for 5–10 minutes.

✱ Crêpes can be filled with all manner of sweet fillings, including fruit compotes (see pages 21–25) and ice creams (see page 126).

1 Pouring the beaten egg into the flour well.

2 Gradually incorporating the flour into the egg.

3 Stirring a little of the milk into the mixture to loosen it.

4 Checking that the batter is at the correct 'thin cream' consistency for making crêpes.

(Continued overleaf)

5 Lightly greasing the pan using kitchen paper dipped in melted butter.

6 Swirling the pan to cover the bottom with a thin layer of batter.

7 Lifting the edge of the crêpe with a palette knife to check the colour on the underside.

8 Turning the crêpe over in the pan. Once cooked on both sides the crêpes are stacked, interleaved with greaseproof paper.

CARAMELISED BANOFFEE CRÊPES

SERVES 4

8 warm crêpes
   (see page 64)

FOR THE TOFFEE SAUCE
70g unsalted butter
70g demerara sugar
1 tsp golden syrup
1½ tsp black treacle
200ml double cream

FOR THE FILLING
4 small, ripe bananas
40g unsalted butter
40g caster sugar
1 tbsp lemon juice

TO FINISH (OPTIONAL)
Icing sugar, to dust

This is a lovely incarnation of the ever-popular banana and toffee partnership. The pancakes can be made in advance and reheated in a warm oven before filling with the banana mixture.

1 To make the toffee sauce, put the butter and demerara sugar in a small, heavy-based saucepan. Place over a low heat and stir gently until melted. Stir in the golden syrup and treacle. Increase the heat to high, bring to the boil and boil for 1–2 minutes until it reaches a dark caramel colour. Carefully pour in the cream (it will splutter) and stir well to combine. Remove the pan from the heat and keep warm.

2 For the filling, peel the bananas and cut into slices on the diagonal, about 6–8 slices from each banana.

3 Melt the butter in a large sauté or frying pan over a low to medium heat and, when foaming, add the caster sugar. Cook over a medium heat, stirring with a wooden spoon, until lightly caramelised. Stir in the lemon juice, then add the banana slices and shake the pan gently to coat them with the caramel. Remove from the heat and keep warm.

4 Lay the crêpes on a work surface, with the side that was cooked first downwards. Divide the caramel banana mixture between the crêpes. Fold each in half and then in half again to make a triangle.

5 Pour some of the warm toffee sauce onto each of 4 individual serving plates and place 2 crêpes on top of each pool of sauce. Sift a little icing sugar over the crêpes, if you like. Serve with crème fraîche, offering the remaining toffee sauce separately.

A note on branding crêpes...

✲ To make a decorative branding pattern on the crêpes, using oven gloves or a thick oven cloth to protect your hands, heat the lower two thirds of 3 or 4 long metal skewers over a naked flame, until red hot. It is important to heat the skewers evenly, so it may be necessary to turn them in the flame occasionally. Carefully press a hot skewer onto the icing sugar coated surface of the crêpe and hold it there for a few seconds. The intense, direct heat of the metal will cook the icing sugar instantly, creating a golden brown, crisp textured branding mark. Continue the process at intervals, to form several parallel lines across the crêpe. Repeat the process on the reverse diagonal to form a cross hatch or diamond pattern. Use a clean, very hot, skewer after every 2 or 3 brandings, returning used ones to the flame frequently to reheat. Warm or cool skewers will simply melt the sugar and not caramelise it.

3

CREAMY DESSERTS

For sheer indulgence, choose from the tempting range of rich and creamy puddings in this chapter, from tangy fruit fools and creamy mousses, through pannacotta and chilled soufflés to irresistible roulades and cheesecakes.

Whole eggs, or sometimes just the yolks, are used to set creamy custard desserts such as crème brûlée – whole eggs setting a mixture firmly and yolks giving a softer, richer set. Egg dishes must be cooked gently or they will have at best a rubbery texture and at worst the curdled texture of scrambled eggs. To counter this, many dishes are cooked using a hot water bath, called a bain marie, so that the eggs are protected from the fierce oven heat by the water.

WHISKING CREAM

When cream is whisked, air bubbles are trapped, thickening the cream so that it can be used to lighten and enrich mixtures, even helping them to set. Both whipping cream and double cream can be successfully whisked. Care must be taken to avoid over-whisking, which gives the cream an unpleasant grainy, fatty, texture. Make sure the cream is cold before you whisk it, and on a hot day, whisk cream slowly, as it can suddenly thicken.

If you are adding sweetness and flavourings to cream, such as icing or caster sugar, vanilla seeds or grated orange zest, add them before you start whisking. If added at the end, the cream is more likely to become over-whisked. If you add acid or alcohol to cream, it will thicken much faster than usual.

SOFT PEAK Cream whisked to this stage is thick enough to form peaks that hold briefly as you lift the whisk, then dissipate back into the cream. This is usually the required consistency if it is to be folded into another mixture, such as crème pâtissière.

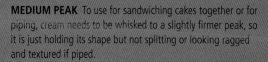

MEDIUM PEAK To use for sandwiching cakes together or for piping, cream needs to be whisked to a slightly firmer peak, so it is just holding its shape but not splitting or looking ragged and textured if piped.

PIPING CONSISTENCY When piping whisked cream, it may overheat in a piping bag held by warm hands, and the last of the cream may curdle before it is piped. To avoid this, slightly under-whisk the cream, or only half-fill the piping bag.

RHUBARB FOOL

300g rhubarb (about
    2–3 thin sticks)
150ml water
100g caster sugar
½ vanilla pod

300ml whole milk
3 egg yolks
1 tbsp cornflour
150ml double cream
A little icing sugar, to taste

If you can restrain yourself from stirring the 3 elements of this rhubarb fool together completely in the final step, you can achieve a lovely 'rhubarb ripple' effect which looks particularly good served in glasses.

1 Trim the ends off the rhubarb, cut into 3cm pieces and put into a saucepan with the water. Cover and cook over a low heat for about 20 minutes until the rhubarb has completely softened. Stir in half of the sugar and simmer, uncovered, until all but about 2 tbsp of the liquid has evaporated. Take off the heat and leave to cool.

2 Meanwhile, make the custard. Split the half vanilla pod lengthways, put into a saucepan with the milk and bring to scalding point (see page 155). Beat the yolks and cornflour with the remaining sugar in a bowl until smooth.

3 Gradually stir in the hot milk, reserving the vanilla pod, then pour the custard back into the rinsed out pan and return to a medium heat. Stir with a wooden spoon until the custard comes to the boil.

4 Remove from the heat and scrape the seeds out of the vanilla pod into the custard. Strain into a bowl and cover the surface with cling film to prevent a skin from forming as it cools.

5 When the rhubarb and custard are both cool, lightly whip the cream to the soft peak stage (see left).

6 Stir the rhubarb into the custard, then fold in the cream. Taste and add icing sugar if needed. Spoon into tall glasses to serve.

Variations

✽ **Gooseberry and elderflower fool** Replace the rhubarb with 300g gooseberries, adding 75ml elderflower cordial in place of the sugar once the gooseberries are soft. Push the fruit through a sieve to make a purée before cooling and adding it to the custard and cream. Add more cordial or icing sugar to sweeten if required.

✽ **Quick summer berry fool** Omit the rhubarb. Mash 300g mixed summer berries with 50g caster sugar and mix with the custard and cream.

CLASSIC CRÈME BRÛLÉE

SERVES 4

300ml double cream
1 vanilla pod
4 egg yolks

1–2 tbsp caster sugar,
to taste, plus extra for
the topping

Ideally, you should start preparing this dish a day in advance to allow time for chilling. You will need 4 ramekins; alternatively, you can use classic 'ear dishes' (see note).

1 Heat the oven to 150°C/gas mark 2.

2 Put the cream into a saucepan. Split the vanilla pod in half lengthways, scrape out the seeds and add them to the cream along with the pod. Bring to scalding point (see page 155) over a low to medium heat. Remove from the heat and leave the vanilla to infuse for at least 10 minutes, then remove and discard the pod.

3 Mix the egg yolks with the sugar in a medium bowl, then pour the warm cream into the bowl and stir until combined.

4 Strain the custard into 4 ramekins. Stand them in a roasting tin. Pour in enough boiling water to come half to three quarters of the way up the sides of the dishes. Transfer to the oven and cook for 30–40 minutes, or until just set and a skin has formed. Leave to cool and then chill in the fridge overnight, to allow them to set further.

5 For the topping, use either a kitchen blowtorch or the grill heated to its highest setting. Sprinkle an even 2–3mm layer of caster sugar over each custard (as shown). Wipe the rim of the dish to remove any excess sugar, to avoid it burning. Spraying the sugar very lightly with water, using a spray bottle, can speed up the caramelising process, helping the sugar to dissolve. If using a blowtorch to caramelise the sugar (as shown), avoid holding the torch too close to the sugar and keep it moving to avoid burnt patches. If placing the ramekins under the grill, move the dishes as necessary to achieve an even colour.

6 Leave the caramel to cool and serve within 1 hour. Do not chill or the caramel will liquefy.

Variations

✴ **Coffee crème brûlée** Omit the vanilla pod. Add 1–2 tsp instant coffee granules to the cream when scalding, allowing it to melt into the cream. Proceed as for the main recipe.

✴ **White chocolate and Earl Grey tea crème brûlée** Omit the vanilla pod and infuse the cream when scalding with 1 tsp Earl Grey tea leaves, or to taste; it shouldn't be too strong. Strain the cream and discard the tea. Reheat the cream, adding 30g white chocolate, in pieces. Allow the chocolate to melt fully in the cream, then proceed as for the main recipe.

✴ **Stem ginger crème brûlée** Omit the vanilla pod. Cut a ball of preserved stem ginger into julienne and add to the cream when scalding. In place of the 1–2 tbsp sugar, use syrup from the jar of preserved ginger to taste.

✴ **Orange crème brûlée** Omit the vanilla pod and infuse the scalding cream with the finely pared zest of 1 orange, then strain and proceed as for the main recipe. A few drops of Grand Marnier or orange flower water can be added to the custard, before straining, to taste. It might also be necessary to add an extra 1–2 tsp caster sugar, to taste.

✴ **Cinnamon crème brûlée** Omit the vanilla pod and infuse the scalded cream with 2–3 cinnamon sticks for 30 minutes. Remove the cinnamon and proceed as for the main recipe.

A note on using 'ear dishes'...

✴ Use the traditional shallow 'ear dishes' (125ml capacity) if you have them; the custard will probably cook more quickly, so check after 20–30 minutes.

STOVETOP CRÈME BRÛLÉE

SERVES 4–6

500ml double cream
1 vanilla pod
8 egg yolks

80g caster sugar
4–6 tbsp demerara sugar

This method of making crème brûlée involves cooking the custard until thick on the stove rather than the more traditional method of slow cooking in the oven, and gives a particularly velvety texture. Ideally, you would start to prepare this dish a day in advance. You will need 4 traditional custard 'ear dishes', or other shallow individual gratin dishes.

1 Place the custard dishes on a baking sheet in the fridge to chill. Pour the cream into a medium saucepan. Cut the vanilla pod in half lengthways, scrape out the seeds and put the pods and seeds into the cream. Place over a medium heat and bring to scalding point (see page 155). Remove from the heat and leave to infuse for at least 5 minutes, but ideally 20–30 minutes for a more pronounced vanilla flavour.

2 Place the egg yolks in a medium bowl, add the caster sugar and mix well to combine.

3 Place a fine sieve over a separate medium bowl and set aside. Meanwhile, reheat the infused cream. Gradually pour small amounts of the hot cream over the yolk mixture in the bowl, stirring until it has all been incorporated. Rinse out the pan.

4 Return the mixture to the clean pan and place over a medium to low heat. It is very important to stir the mixture slowly and constantly with a wooden spoon to prevent it from curdling. Continue to stir and heat; as the temperature rises the cream will begin to steam and start to thicken. It is cooked when the mixture has thickened considerably, resembling the consistency of natural yoghurt, with the vanilla seeds suspended within. Immediately strain through the sieve into the bowl.

5 Remove the dishes from the fridge and divide the brûlée mixture evenly between them. Return to the fridge for 24 hours, uncovered to encourage them to develop a slight skin.

6 Remove the dishes from the fridge, one by one, 10 minutes before serving, and sprinkle 1–1½ tbsp demerara sugar over the surface of each, tilting and tapping the dish to ensure an even covering of sugar across the top.

7 Use a cook's blowtorch to caramelise the topping to a deep golden brown. Alternatively, you can place the dishes under the grill to colour. Return the brûlées to the fridge for 5–10 minutes before serving, to allow the caramel to cool and set quickly, so that it has a proper crack when tapped with a spoon.

Using a digital thermometer...

✳ If you have a digital thermometer, hold the probe with the same hand as the heatproof spatula or wooden spoon with which you are stirring; this will provide you with a reliable reading of the temperature of the mixture. Stir the mixture until it reaches 84°C for the perfect set. However, if you don't have such equipment at home, don't worry, the recipe above describes what to look for when making the custard without.

CRÈME CARAMEL

SERVES 6

100g granulated sugar
4 tbsp water
600ml whole milk

Few drops of vanilla extract
4 eggs
2 tbsp caster sugar

You need to prepare this dish a day in advance, to allow time for it to set properly. You will need a 1 litre ovenproof dish, 4–5cm deep.

1 Heat the oven to 150°C/gas mark 2 and place the ovenproof dish in the oven to warm up.

2 Put the granulated sugar and water into a heavy-based saucepan and heat gently until the sugar has dissolved. Using a pastry brush dipped in water, brush down the sides of the pan (see page 142) and bring the syrup to a gentle simmer. Simmer until it caramelises and reaches a rich golden colour, then immediately remove from the heat.

3 Working quickly and wearing oven gloves to protect your hands, remove the dish from the oven and pour in the caramel. Immediately tip and rotate the dish so that the caramel coats the insides evenly. Set aside.

4 Pour the milk into a saucepan, place over a low to medium heat and bring to scalding point (see page 155), then remove from the heat and stir in the vanilla extract.

5 Mix the eggs and caster sugar in a large bowl until well combined, but avoid introducing too many air bubbles. Gradually pour the milk into the egg mixture, stirring well, then strain the custard into the prepared dish. Cover with foil to prevent a thick skin from forming when cooking.

6 Half-fill a roasting tin with boiling water to make a bain marie. Place the dish in the tin, making sure the water comes about half to three quarters up the sides of the dish.

7 Carefully transfer the tin to the bottom third of the oven and cook for 60–75 minutes, or until the centre is just set. There will be a uniform (but not violent) wobble to the custard when it is jiggled gently, but it will no longer be liquid. (The custard will firm up once it is cool.)

8 Leave the crème caramel to cool, then place in the fridge to chill overnight.

9 To serve, remove the crème caramel from the fridge at least 30 minutes before serving, to bring it to room temperature, as the flavour will be better. Ease the top edge of the custard away from the dish using only the very tip of a small knife. Invert a plate over the dish then, holding on to the dish and the plate, turn the plate the right way up with the dish now upside down. The crème caramel should drop down onto the plate. Carefully lift away the dish.

Variation

✳ **Rum and raisin crème caramel** Put 50g raisins in a saucepan with 4 tbsp dark rum and 4 tbsp water. Bring to the boil, remove from the heat and set aside for 20 minutes to plump up. Drain the raisins, reserving the liquor. Make the liquor up to 4 tbsp (it doesn't matter if it is a little more) with more rum, and use in place of the water to make the caramel. Replace 50ml of the milk in the custard with 50ml dark rum. Once the dish has been lined with the caramel, sprinkle over the soaked raisins before you strain over the custard. Proceed as for the main recipe.

For individual crème caramels...

✳ If using individual ramekins, this quantity will serve about 6, and will take less time to cook, about 40–50 minutes. You will need to work very quickly when dividing the caramel between the ramekins.

CHERRY CLAFOUTIS

SERVES 4	
350–400g sweet black cherries	4 eggs
4 tbsp Kirsch	120–140g caster sugar, to taste, plus extra to sprinkle
½ vanilla pod	20g plain flour
150ml whole milk	Pinch of salt
100ml double cream	10g butter, to grease

This classic, simple dish can be adapted to use pretty much any soft fruit in season (see variations). Using fruit that has a certain amount of acidity – the slightly sourer varieties of cherry, for example – will provide a lovely contrast to the creamy batter. You will need a 1–1.25 litre ovenproof dish, 3–4cm deep.

1 Heat the oven to 180°C/gas mark 4.

2 Remove the stones from the cherries using a cherry or olive stoner. Place the cherries in a bowl and sprinkle over the Kirsch.

3 Split the half vanilla pod lengthways and put it into a small saucepan with the milk and cream. Bring to scalding point (see page 155), then remove the pan from the heat and set aside to infuse for at least 10 minutes.

4 Put the eggs and sugar into a medium bowl and whisk until the mixture is light and creamy. Add the flour and salt and whisk again until smooth.

5 Remove the vanilla pod from the milk and scrape the seeds back into the milk. Strain the infused milk onto the egg mixture and whisk well.

6 Use the butter to grease the ovenproof dish and sprinkle it with caster sugar. Scatter the cherries over the bottom of the dish, discarding the remaining Kirsch, then pour over the batter.

7 Cook in the middle of the oven for 50–60 minutes. The clafoutis should be slightly risen and browning round the edges, but although set, the mixture will still be a little softer in the centre. Sprinkle with caster sugar and serve with a cherry compote or with clotted cream, or both.

Variations

✳ **Apricot clafoutis** Replace the Kirsch with 2 tbsp Amaretto liqueur. Halve 8 small, ripe apricots, remove the stones and place, cut side down, in the dish, instead of the cherries. Alternatively, use 1 quantity poached apricots (see page 20, omitting the cardamom).

✳ **Blueberry clafoutis** Replace the cherries with 300–350g blueberries and the Kirsch with 2 tbsp Amaretto liqueur. Add the finely grated zest of ½ lemon to the batter, if you like.

✳ **Blackberry clafoutis** Replace the cherries and Kirsch with 300g blackberries and 4 tbsp crème de mûres. If the blackberries are very sharp, add a little more sugar.

✳ **Plum clafoutis** Halve 8 small, ripe plums, remove the stones and place, cut side down, in the dish, instead of the cherries. Add a good pinch of ground cinnamon or a very finely diced ball of preserved stem ginger to the batter, if you like.

✳ **Prune clafoutis** Soak 200g prunes overnight in a mixture of 50ml brandy and 150ml apple juice and use in place of the cherries, discarding any remaining soaking juices.

For individual clafoutis...

✳ Use four 15cm gratin dishes and bake for 20–25 minutes.

PAIN PERDU WITH BUTTERSCOTCH APRICOTS

SERVES 4

FOR THE BUTTERSCOTCH APRICOTS
85g unsalted butter
85g soft light brown sugar
6 ripe apricots
2 tbsp apricot brandy
75ml double cream

FOR THE CUSTARD
1 large egg, plus 1 extra yolk
50g soft light brown sugar

150ml whole milk
1 tbsp apricot brandy
  (optional)

TO ASSEMBLE
4 slices of day-old brioche
  or white bread, cut
  2.5cm thick
50g unsalted butter
Caster sugar, to sprinkle

There are many variations of this simple recipe, also known as poor knight's pudding, French toast or simply eggy bread. This is a more sophisticated version, but could easily be adapted for a quick snack or impromptu Sunday brunch, by replacing the apricot brandy in the custard with fruit juice, and serving with a few fresh berries or a fruit compote in place of the rich butterscotch apricots.

1 To make the butterscotch sauce, put the butter and sugar in a wide, shallow frying pan large enough to hold the apricots (once halved) in a single layer. Place the pan over a low heat and once the butter has started to melt, stir with a wooden spoon until fully melted and the sugar has dissolved.

2 Cut the apricots in half and remove the stones. Place cut side down in the pan and cook gently, basting occasionally with the hot butter mixture, until just tender when pierced with the tip of a sharp knife; about 5 minutes depending on their ripeness.

3 Increase the heat to medium, pour in the apricot brandy and cook for a further minute, or until the apricots are just beginning to caramelise a little around the edges. Carefully

pour in the cream, (it will splutter) and bring to the boil. Turn the apricots in the hot sauce to coat them evenly, remove the pan from the heat and keep warm.

4 To make the custard, put the egg, extra yolk and sugar into a medium bowl and beat together with a wooden spoon, to combine. Stir in the milk and apricot brandy. Strain the custard through a sieve into a large, shallow dish.

5 Cut each slice of brioche into 2 triangles. Lay them in the dish, in a single layer, and leave to soak up the custard for 5 minutes, turning them over once or twice.

6 Melt half the butter in a large frying pan over a medium heat and, when foaming, fry half the soaked brioche until golden brown on both sides. Drain on kitchen paper and sprinkle with a little caster sugar. Wipe the pan clean and repeat with the remaining butter and brioche.

7 To serve, place 2 triangles of fried brioche attractively on each of 4 individual serving plates. Place 3 apricot halves on each serving and spoon over a little of the warm butterscotch sauce. Serve immediately.

PANETTONE PUDDING

SERVES 4

50g butter, at room
    temperature
4–5 even slices of panettone,
    cut 7–8mm thick
30g piece of good quality
    candied citrus peel
2 eggs, plus 1 extra yolk
40–50g caster sugar, to taste

Few drops of vanilla extract
560ml whole milk
2–3 tbsp Amaretto liqueur
1–2 tbsp demerara sugar,
    to sprinkle
Freshly grated nutmeg or
    ground cinnamon

This is a lovely version of bread and butter pudding, using the traditional Italian festive loaf, which is usually studded with dried or crystallised fruit. It is a great way to use up any slightly stale panettone as the drier slices will soak up the custard really well. You will need a 1 litre ovenproof dish, 4–5cm deep.

1 Use a little of the butter to grease the ovenproof dish.

2 Butter the panettone slices and cut roughly into triangular quarters. Finely chop the candied peel. Layer the panettone and chopped peel in the buttered dish, finishing with a layer of panettone and arranging the slices at an angle rather than flat. This will help the edges of the panettone to crisp and colour.

3 Mix the eggs, extra yolk, sugar and vanilla extract together in a jug, then pour in the milk and Amaretto, stirring well. Strain this custard mixture over the panettone, gently pushing the pieces down into the custard to ensure they are fully coated. (The panettone does not have to be completely covered with custard, but the top layer should have soaked some up.) Set aside to soak for up to 30 minutes.

4 Heat the oven to 150°C/gas mark 2. Sprinkle the demerara sugar and a pinch of nutmeg or cinnamon over the surface of the pudding.

5 Half-fill a roasting tin with hot water to make a bain marie and stand the dish in the tin. Transfer to the middle of the oven and cook for about 1¼–1½ hours, or until the custard is just set but still slightly runny in the middle and the top is brown and crusty. If it has not taken on colour, place under a hot grill for a very short time, less than a minute, to brown a little.

Variation

✳ **Classic bread and butter pudding** Replace the panettone with good quality white bread and use 2 tbsp sultanas or raisins in place of the candied peel. Omit the Amaretto liqueur and use an extra 2–3 tbsp milk.

MANGO
MOUSSE

SERVES 6

400g tin evaporated milk
8–10 ripe mangoes, or an
   850g tin mango pulp
1 lime

About 100g caster sugar
150ml cold water
3 tsp powdered gelatine

. . . .

This recipe is from Priya Wickramasinghe, who has been sharing her knowledge of Indian and Sri Lankan food with our students for many years. Priya recommends using Alphonso mangoes when available, but is happy to use tinned mango pulp if necessary. The tinned pulp can be very sweet, so you will need to adjust the sugar accordingly. The evaporated milk needs to be simmered and frozen the day before you want to serve the mousse.

1 Place the unopened tin of evaporated milk in a saucepan and cover with cold water so that it is completely submerged. Bring to the boil, then turn down the heat and simmer for 20 minutes, making sure that the water is topped up and the tin remains submerged. Allow the tin to cool, then place it in the freezer overnight.

2 Peel the mangoes and remove the stones. Cut the flesh into chunks and place in a blender. Juice the lime and add the juice to the mango along with half of the sugar. Blend to a smooth purée, taste and blend in more sugar if needed.

3 Put the cold water into a small pan. Sprinkle over the gelatine and leave for 5 minutes to sponge, then place the pan over a low heat and heat gently, without boiling, until the gelatine has dissolved, stirring as little as possible (see page 36).

4 Tip the contents of the tin of chilled evaporated milk into a large bowl. Roughly chop it into pieces, then use a hand-held electric whisk to whisk it until light and frothy. Whisk in the mango purée and then enough sugar to sweeten the mixture to your taste. Continue to whisk until well mixed.

5 Add the liquid gelatine, mix well and pour the mousse into a large glass bowl or individual dishes. Refrigerate for at least 3 hours before serving.

. . . .

A note on using gelatine to set creamy mixtures...

✱ Just follow the guidelines on page 92 and remember to get the mousses out of the fridge 20–30 minutes before you serve them to soften a little.

CHOCOLATE MOUSSE

SERVES 4

100g good quality
   dark chocolate, about
   60% cocoa solids

4 eggs

A classic chocolate mousse contains just chocolate and eggs so this is a good excuse to try out the many interesting artisan chocolates available now. We find a chocolate of about 60% cocoa solids gives the best flavour balance to this mousse.

1 Chop the chocolate up into small pieces and place in a heatproof bowl. Bring a small pan of water up to boiling point, then remove it from the heat and place the bowl of chocolate on top, making sure the bowl isn't in direct contact with the water. Allow the chocolate to melt, stirring occasionally, then remove the bowl from the pan and set aside to cool a little.

2 Separate the eggs into 2 medium bowls (see page 56). Whisk the whites to medium-stiff peaks (see page 109).

3 Stir the cooled melted chocolate into the egg yolks until evenly combined.

4 Using a large metal spoon or rubber spatula, stir a large spoonful of the egg whites into the mixture to loosen it, then carefully fold in the remainder of the egg whites (as shown).

5 Divide the mousse between 4 individual serving dishes or glasses and wipe away any drips.

6 Chill for at least 4 hours before serving. The mousse can be served as it is, or decorated with chocolate curls or raspberries.

Variations

✱ You can flavour the chocolate with a little liqueur: Amaretto, Kahlua, Irish cream, brandy, Cointreau and crème de menthe work particularly well: add ½ tsp of the liqueur to the chocolate after it has melted. Alternatively, flavour the chocolate with 8–10 drops of flavoured oil, such as mint, bitter orange or basil, adding the oil to the chocolate before melting.

VANILLA PANNACOTTA

SERVES 4

1 tsp oil, to grease
400ml double cream
¼–½ vanilla pod
1 pared strip of lemon zest
60–75g caster sugar
2½ sheets of leaf gelatine
200ml whole milk, at room temperature

TO SERVE
Fruit compote such as rhubarb and vanilla (see page 21), or roasted fruit such as honey and thyme roasted figs (see page 16), or fresh berries

Pannacotta translates as cooked cream, and here a cream subtly infused with the flavour of vanilla, is lightly set with gelatine. You will need 4 individual 150ml capacity pudding moulds.

1 Brush the pudding moulds very lightly with oil; invert on a wire rack to drain.

2 Put the cream into a saucepan with the vanilla pod and lemon zest, then bring to scalding point over a medium heat (see page 155). Remove from the heat, add 60g sugar and stir to dissolve. Set aside to infuse for 15–20 minutes.

3 Soak the gelatine in cold water until soft, about 5 minutes (see page 38).

4 Remove the vanilla and lemon zest from the infused cream and gently reheat over a low to medium heat. Squeeze the excess water out of the gelatine, then add the gelatine sheets to the warmed cream, stirring to dissolve. Strain the mixture into a bowl and add the milk. Taste and add a little more sugar if needed (there should still be enough heat in the mixture to dissolve it).

5 Pour the mixture into the moulds and chill in the fridge for a few hours, or ideally overnight.

6 About 20 minutes before serving, take the pannacottas out of the fridge. To turn out, dip the moulds (to the rim), in warm water for 5 seconds, then remove and gently release the pannacotta from the mould using a fingertip. (Don't leave them in the water any longer or the pannacotta will melt.) Invert onto a plate and, while holding the mould and the plate, give a good sideways shake to release the pannacotta. Serve with a fruit compote, roasted fruit or berries.

Variations

✻ For an even richer flavour, omit the milk and use 600ml double cream.

✻ Cardamom pannacotta Replace the vanilla with ½–1 tsp crushed cardamom seeds. Proceed as for the main recipe.

✻ Rosewater pannacotta Omit the vanilla and add ½ tsp rosewater to the pannacotta with the milk.

ROASTED ALMOND PANNACOTTA

SERVES 4

Sunflower oil, to grease
200g flaked almonds
125ml whole milk
500ml double cream
70g caster sugar

Pinch of salt
1½ sheets of leaf gelatine
4 tsp Pedro Ximenez sherry,
　to serve (optional)

Either serve these pannacottas turned out onto a plate with some fresh raspberries or a fruit compote, or set them in glasses and serve with a teaspoon of Pedro Ximenez sherry poured on top. You will need 4 individual 150ml capacity pudding moulds or glasses.

1 Heat the oven to 180°C/gas mark 4. Brush the pudding moulds, if using, lightly with oil; invert onto a wire rack to drain.

2 Spread the flaked almonds out on a baking sheet and toast in the oven for 8–10 minutes until they are evenly deep golden in colour; watch carefully as they can darken quickly.

3 Meanwhile, pour the milk and cream into a saucepan, stir in the sugar and salt and bring to a simmer. Add the toasted almonds while they are still hot, take off the heat and leave to infuse for 30 minutes (no longer or the nuts will soak up too much of the liquid).

4 Strain the infused mixture through a fine sieve into a saucepan, using a ladle to push though as much liquid as possible; discard the almonds. Bring the mixture up to scalding point (see page 155), then remove from the heat.

5 Place the gelatine in a bowl and cover with cold water. Leave to soak for 5 minutes until soft (see page 38).

6 Squeeze the excess water out of the gelatine, then add the gelatine sheets to the warmed cream infusion and stir to dissolve. Strain the mixture through a sieve into a jug.

7 Pour into glasses or the oiled moulds and chill in the fridge for a few hours, or ideally overnight.

8 Half an hour before serving, take the pannacottas out of the fridge. If you are turning them out, dip the moulds (to the rim), in warm water for up to 5 seconds, then remove and gently release the top edge of the pannacotta from the mould using a fingertip. (Don't leave them in the water for any longer than necessary or the pannacotta will melt.) Invert onto a plate and, while holding the mould and the plate, give a good sideways shake to release the pannacotta. Carefully remove the mould. Serve trickled with a little Pedro Ximenez, if you like.

CARAMEL PANNACOTTA WITH NUTTY CROQUANT

<table>
<tr><td colspan="2">SERVES 4</td></tr>
<tr><td>FOR THE PANNACOTTA</td><td>FOR THE CROQUANT</td></tr>
<tr><td>Sunflower oil, to grease</td><td>85g flaked almonds</td></tr>
<tr><td>500ml double cream</td><td>100g caster sugar</td></tr>
<tr><td>100ml whole milk</td><td>1 tsp liquid glucose</td></tr>
<tr><td>2½ sheets of leaf gelatine</td><td></td></tr>
<tr><td>110g caster sugar</td><td></td></tr>
<tr><td>3 tbsp water</td><td></td></tr>
</table>

The croquant is a piece of almond praline or brittle that can be cut into all manner of dramatic shapes if you are cooking to impress. Any left over can be bashed with a rolling pin into small pieces and sprinkled over ice cream. You will need 4 individual 150ml capacity pudding moulds or ramekins.

1 Brush the pudding moulds or ramekins very lightly with oil and invert onto a wire rack to drain.

2 Pour the cream and milk into a saucepan, place over a medium heat and bring to scalding point (see page 155). Strain through a sieve into a jug, to remove any skin, and set aside while you soak the gelatine and make the caramel.

3 Place the gelatine in a bowl and cover with cold water. Leave to soak for 5 minutes until soft (see page 38).

4 Next make the caramel. Put the sugar and water into a medium saucepan and dissolve over a gentle heat. Once the sugar had dissolved, increase the heat and bring to the boil until it caramelises and takes on a deep golden colour. You may need to swirl the caramel to encourage even colouring.

5 As soon as the caramel has reached an even deep golden colour, take the pan off the heat and carefully pour in the cream mixture (it will splutter). Return the pan to the heat to melt any lumps by stirring with a wooden spoon, if necessary.

6 Squeeze the excess water out of the gelatine, then add the gelatine to the hot caramel cream, stirring to dissolve.

7 Strain the mixture through a sieve into the prepared moulds and chill in the fridge for a few hours, or ideally overnight.

8 To make the croquant, heat the oven to 180°C/gas mark 4. Lightly oil a baking sheet. Spread the flaked almonds out on a second baking sheet and toast in the oven until pale golden brown, 5–8 minutes, then remove and keep warm.

9 Meanwhile, put the sugar and liquid glucose into a heavy-based sauté or frying pan and set over a low heat. As the sugar begins to take on colour, use a fork to gently encourage the unmelted sugar to the edges of the pan to achieve an even colouring. When all the sugar has caramelised to a deep amber colour, add the still warm nuts and turn to coat in the caramel.

10 Tip the mixture onto the oiled baking sheet and turn it over with a lightly oiled palette knife. While still warm and pliable, roll it as thinly as possible, using a rolling pin. Once cool, cut into triangles or any other desired shape, using a sharp knife.

11 Remove the pannacottas from the fridge 30 minutes before serving. To turn out, dip the moulds (to the rim) in warm water for 5 seconds, then gently release the top edge of the pannacotta from the mould using a fingertip. Invert onto individual serving plates and, holding the mould and the plate, give a good sideways shake to release the pannacotta. Carefully remove the mould and serve with the almond croquant.

VANILLA BAVAROIS

SERVES 4

1 tsp sunflower oil, to grease
300ml double cream
300ml whole milk
1 vanilla pod
1½ sheets of leaf gelatine
4 egg yolks
60–75g caster sugar

TO SERVE
Fruit compote such as
 blackberry and lemon
 (see page 25), or roasted
 fruit such as honey and
 thyme roasted figs (see
 page 16), or fresh berries

A bavarois is a custard or crème anglaise that is flavoured and set with gelatine. This is the classic vanilla flavoured bavarois. Serve with a spoonful of compote made with whatever fruit is in season. You will need 4 darioles or individual glass moulds.

1 Very lightly oil the 4 moulds and place a disc of non-stick baking parchment in the bottom of each (to ensure an easy release when unmoulding the bavarois). Lightly whisk the cream in a bowl and set aside in the fridge until needed.

2 Pour the milk into a saucepan. Split the vanilla pod in half lengthways, scrape the seeds out into the milk and add the pod. Bring the milk slowly to scalding point (see page 155) over a low to medium heat, then remove from the heat and leave to infuse for about 15 minutes.

3 Meanwhile, put the gelatine sheets in a bowl, cover with cold water and leave to soften for 5–10 minutes (see page 38).

4 In a separate bowl, mix the egg yolks and 60g sugar together. Pour the flavoured milk onto the egg yolks, stirring, then return the mixture to the rinsed out saucepan. Taste for sweetness and add a little more sugar if required. Discard the vanilla pod.

5 Stir the mixture continuously with a wooden spoon over a low to medium heat, until it thickens enough to evenly coat the back of the spoon (see page 146) and becomes a thin custard. Remove from the heat.

6 Remove the gelatine from the water, squeeze out any excess water and add the gelatine leaves to the warm custard. Stir gently to dissolve the gelatine, then pass the mixture through a fine sieve into a bowl.

7 Place the bowl over an ice bath and bring the mixture to setting point (see page 92). The custard must come to setting point to hold the vanilla seeds in suspension. Remove the bowl from the ice bath and gently fold the lightly whipped cream into the mixture.

8 Pour the bavarois mixture into the prepared moulds and chill in the fridge for a few hours until set, or overnight.

9 To unmould the bavarois, suspend the moulds in warm water just to the rim for 5 seconds (as shown); this is just enough time to melt the surface of the bavarois. Remove and gently release the bavarois using the tip of your finger or thumb (as shown). Invert onto a serving plate and, while holding the mould and the plate, give everything a good sideways shake (as shown); this should release the bavarois from the mould. Wipe away any melted bavarois as cleanly as possible, using dampened kitchen paper. Serve with a fruit compote, roasted fruit or berries.

Variations

✳ **Chocolate bavarois** Omit the vanilla and add 100g good quality dark chocolate, chopped into small pieces, to the cold milk. Stir over a low heat until melted, then proceed as for the main recipe. Adding chocolate gives a firmer set.

✳ **Mocha bavarois** Omit the vanilla and add 1½ tbsp instant coffee granules and 40g good quality dark chocolate, chopped into small pieces, to the cold milk. Stir over a low heat until melted, then proceed as for the main recipe.

COLD SOUFFLÉS

Cold soufflés bear little relation to their hot namesake. Traditionally they are served in the same soufflé dishes or individual ramekins as hot soufflés and made to resemble them by the crafty means of tying a strip of greaseproof paper around the top of the dish and pouring in the mixture to the top of the paper to set. When the paper is removed, the cold soufflé appears to have risen above the rim of the dish just as for a hot soufflé.

Cold soufflés are actually just light and airy mousses that are sometimes set with gelatine. Nowadays they are often set and presented in a glass serving dish or pretty individual dishes rather than in the traditional way.

All manner of fruits – and chocolate – can be used to flavour these desserts and they have the advantage that they can be prepared well ahead.

TECHNIQUE
SETTING POINT FOR COLD SOUFFLÉS, MOUSSES, ETC.

A liquid or mixture with gelatine in it must be brought to 'setting point' (over an ice bath for speed), so it can combine with a foamy mixture without separating. Whipped cream, whisked egg whites or a mousse of yolks may be added to a gelatine mixture, to create volume and lightness in the finished dish. The gelatine also prevents other ingredients sinking to the bottom, such as the vanilla seeds in a cold vanilla soufflé.

1 Once you have added the gelatine (either dissolved powdered or sponged leaf gelatine) to the mixture, place it over an ice bath (a larger bowl half-filled with ice cubes and cold water) and begin stirring gently.

2 Stir continuously and gently to ensure an even cooling and setting, until there is a visible thickening, and when a spatula drawn through the middle of the mixture creates a 'parting of the waves' (when the mixture parts briefly, for 3–5 seconds before flooding back together).

3 At setting point, remove the dish from the ice bath and gently fold in the lighter mixture, such as lightly whipped cream or soft/medium peak whisked egg whites.

A note on using a soufflé dish for a cold soufflé...

✱ Tie a double band of lightly oiled greaseproof paper around the top of the dish, to extend about 3cm above the rim with the non-folded edge uppermost. When the soufflé mixture is poured in, it should come about 2.5cm above the rim of the dish.

Once the soufflé is set, heat a palette knife in hot water, dry it and run it between the double sheets of greaseproof paper against the side of the set soufflé. The heat will very slightly melt just enough of the gelatine to enable the paper collar to be removed cleanly.

The exposed raised side of the soufflé can be spread with a thin layer of lightly whipped cream and coated with nibbed toasted almonds to finish.

CHILLED LEMON SOUFFLÉ

SERVES 4

2 large lemons	150ml double cream
1½ tbsp water	2–3 tsp icing sugar (optional)
1½ tsp powdered gelatine	Citrus zest julienne softened
3 eggs	in sugar syrup (see page
150g caster sugar	11), to finish (optional)

You will need a 1–1.2 litre soufflé dish, prepared as described and shown on page 93, or individual glasses.

1 Pour about 5cm water into a large saucepan, bring to the boil over a medium heat, then remove from the heat.

2 Finely grate the zest from the lemons, then juice them. Put the water and 1½ tbsp lemon juice in a small saucepan and sprinkle the gelatine evenly over the surface. Leave for 5 minutes, or until the gelatine has absorbed the water and become spongy (see page 36).

3 Separate the eggs (see page 56), putting the yolks in a medium heatproof bowl with the caster sugar and 1–1½ tbsp lemon juice; put the whites in another bowl.

4 Lightly whip the cream to medium-soft peaks (see page 72) and set aside in the fridge.

5 Sit the bowl with the yolks and sugar over the hot water pan, making sure the base of the bowl is not touching the water. Using a hand-held electric whisk, whisk until the mixture becomes paler in colour and increases in volume a little. Remove from the heat, continue whisking until cool, then whisk in the remaining lemon juice (about 1½–2 tbsp) and the zest.

6 Put the saucepan containing the gelatine over a very low heat and dissolve the gelatine without stirring. An occasional swirl of the mixture helps to see if it has dissolved. Pour the dissolved gelatine into the lemon mousse mixture, stirring as you do so. Place the bowl over an ice bath, stirring gently until it reaches setting point (see page 92). At this stage it will have thickened slightly and the bottom of the bowl will be exposed for several seconds when a spatula is drawn through before the mixture floods back.

7 Remove the bowl from the ice bath and, working efficiently, fold the whipped cream into the lemon mixture.

8 Using an electric whisk, whisk the egg whites to medium peaks (see page 109) and stir one spoonful into the mixture, to loosen it, then fold the remaining whites in carefully, using a large metal spoon. Taste and add a little icing sugar if the mixture seems too tart.

9 Spoon the mixture into the prepared soufflé dish, or into a serving bowl or individual glasses, and chill in the fridge for 2–3 hours before serving. You can decorate the soufflé with citrus zest julienne, if you wish.

Variations

✳ **Chilled lime soufflé** Replace the lemons with 4 limes.

✳ **Chilled raspberry soufflé** Omit the lemon zest and juice. Make a purée using 350g raspberries, heated, sieved and cooled. Dissolve the gelatine in 3 tbsp water and proceed as for the main recipe, adding the raspberry purée at the end of step 5.

✳ **Chilled blood orange soufflé** Use 1 blood orange and ½ lemon in place of the 2 lemons, using the lemon juice and water to dissolve the gelatine and adding the blood orange juice to the egg and sugar mixture at the end of step 5.

CHILLED PASSION FRUIT SOUFFLÉ

SERVES 4

8–10 passion fruit
    (depending on size), plus
    extra to decorate (optional)
1 large lemon
2 tbsp water

1½ tsp powdered gelatine
3 eggs
120g caster sugar
150ml double cream
2–3 tsp icing sugar (optional)

You will need a 1–1.2 litre soufflé dish, prepared as described and shown on page 93, or individual glasses.

1 Halve the passion fruit, scoop out the seeds and juice into a sieve over a bowl and press with the back of a wooden spoon to extract the juice.

2 Pour about a 5cm depth of water into a large saucepan, bring to the boil over a medium heat, then remove from the heat.

3 Finely grate the zest from the lemon, then juice it. Put 2 tbsp water and 1 tbsp lemon juice in a small saucepan and sprinkle the gelatine evenly over the surface. Leave for 5 minutes, or until the gelatine has absorbed the water and become spongy (see page 36).

4 Separate the eggs (see page 56), putting the yolks in a medium heatproof bowl with the caster sugar and 1 tbsp lemon juice; put the whites in another bowl.

5 Lightly whip the cream to medium-soft peaks (see page 72) and set aside in the fridge.

6 Sit the bowl with the yolks and sugar over the hot water pan, making sure the bottom of the bowl is not touching the water. Using a hand-held electric whisk, whisk until the mixture becomes paler in colour and increases in volume a little. Remove from the heat, continue whisking until cool, then whisk in the sieved passion fruit pulp with the lemon zest and any remaining lemon juice.

7 Put the saucepan containing the gelatine over a very low heat and dissolve the gelatine without stirring. An occasional swirl of the mixture helps to see if it has dissolved. Pour the dissolved gelatine into the passion fruit mousse mixture, stirring as you do so. Place the bowl over an ice bath, stirring gently until it reaches setting point (see page 92). At this stage it will have thickened slightly and the bottom of the bowl will be exposed for several seconds when a spatula is drawn through before the mixture floods back.

8 Remove the bowl from the ice bath and, working efficiently, fold the whipped cream into the passion fruit mixture.

9 Using an electric whisk, whisk the egg whites to medium peaks (see page 109) and stir one spoonful into the mixture, to loosen it, then fold the remaining whites in carefully, using a large metal spoon. Taste and add a little icing sugar if the mixture seems too tart.

10 Spoon the mixture into the prepared soufflé dish, or into a serving bowl or individual glasses, and chill in the fridge for 2–3 hours before serving. You can decorate the soufflé with passion fruit seeds if you wish.

CHILLED CHOCOLATE AND HAZELNUT SOUFFLÉ

SERVES 6–8

180g good quality dark chocolate, 70% cocoa solids
3 eggs, plus 1 extra white
30g caster sugar
225ml double cream
2 tbsp Frangelico hazelnut liqueur

FOR THE HAZELNUT PRALINE
Sunflower oil, to grease
150g blanched hazelnuts
150g caster sugar

Served in espresso cups, this irresistible dessert is topped with a hazelnut praline. For a decorative finish, when the praline is cooling but still slightly warm, pull out 8 hazelnuts, one at a time, and they will come away covered in caramel with a shard of caramel attached. Place one on top of each soufflé to serve. You will need 6–8 espresso cups.

1 Place the espresso cups on a tray. Chop the chocolate into small pieces and put into a heatproof bowl set over a saucepan of just-boiled water, ensuring the bowl is not touching the water. Give the chocolate an occasional stir to help it to melt, then remove the bowl from the pan and allow the chocolate to cool slightly.

2 Separate the eggs (see page 56), putting all 4 whites in the same bowl. Add all but 1 tbsp of the sugar to the yolks and beat with a wooden spoon until well combined. Stir the yolk mixture into the melted chocolate.

3 Lightly whip the cream, until it is roughly the same consistency as the chocolate, and fold into the chocolate mixture along with the Frangelico.

4 Whisk the 4 egg whites in a large bowl to medium-stiff peaks (see page 109), then whisk in the reserved 1 tbsp sugar. Fold the egg whites into the chocolate cream mixture, making sure the mixture is a uniform colour with no streaks of egg white.

5 Divide the mixture evenly between the espresso cups and chill in the fridge for at least 2 hours to set, or ideally overnight.

6 To make the hazelnut praline, lightly oil a baking sheet. Put the nuts and sugar into a heavy-based saucepan and heat gently. As the sugar begins to melt, use a fork to gently encourage the unmelted sugar to the sides of the pan, to melt and caramelise.

7 When the sugar is a rich golden colour and the hazelnuts are lightly toasted, tip the mixture out onto the oiled baking sheet and flatten with the fork. Allow to cool completely.

8 Once cooled, coarsely grind the praline using a pestle and mortar or break into pieces by bashing with a rolling pin.

9 Decorate the top of each chilled soufflé with a scattering of hazelnut praline, and serve. Any spare praline can be stored in an airtight container, to be served with good vanilla ice cream.

CHOCOLATE ROULADE

250g good quality dark
   chocolate, about 60%
   cocoa solids
90ml water
1 tsp instant coffee granules

5 eggs
150g caster sugar
2 tbsp icing sugar, plus
   extra to dust
200ml double cream

This roulade is delicious served with fresh raspberries, orange segments or a fruit compote. You will need a 30 x 25cm Swiss roll tin or baking tray.

1 Heat the oven to 200°C/gas mark 6. Line the baking tin with a piece of non-stick baking parchment, 3–4cm bigger on all sides than the tin. Fold the parchment in half and cut diagonally through the corners, about 4–5cm deep. Press into the roasting tin; the cuts in the corners allow it to sit neatly in the tin.

2 Put the chocolate, water and coffee in a small saucepan and melt over a low heat. Remove from the heat and let cool a little.

3 Separate the eggs into 2 medium bowls (see page 56). Using an electric whisk, beat the yolks with all but 1 tbsp of the caster sugar until pale and mousse-like.

4 With clean beaters, whisk the whites to medium-stiff peaks (see page 109), then whisk in the remaining 1 tbsp of caster sugar quickly, to stabilise the whites.

5 Stir the melted, cooled chocolate mixture into the yolk and sugar mixture, just until the mixture is marbled. Stir in one large spoonful of the whites to loosen the mixture, then add the remaining whites and carefully fold in.

6 Spread the mixture into the prepared tin and bake in the upper half of the oven for about 15–20 minutes, or until a crust has formed and it is set in the middle. It will still be spongy when pressed with your fingertips.

7 Remove from the oven, carefully slide the sponge on its baking parchment onto a wire rack and immediately cover with lightly dampened kitchen paper or a damp tea towel to prevent it from drying out. Leave it to cool completely.

8 Place a sheet of greaseproof paper, just bigger than the sponge, on the work surface and sift a fine layer of icing sugar onto it. Turn the sponge onto the icing sugar, using the wire rack and baking parchment to support the sponge, then peel off the parchment.

9 In a large bowl, lightly whisk the cream with the icing sugar, to taste, until it is just holding its shape; it should not be too stiff. Spread it over the cooled sponge, leaving a 1–2cm border around the edges.

10 Make an indentation across the width of the sponge 1cm in from the edge, using a palette knife, then using the greaseproof paper to support the sponge, roll it up like a Swiss roll, removing the greaseproof paper as you do so.

11 Wrap the roulade in the greaseproof paper and chill in the fridge for about 15–20 minutes to firm up slightly.

12 When ready to serve, carefully unwrap the roulade on a board, removing the paper. Trim the ends with a large knife, then carefully place the roulade on a large oblong plate. Sift over a little extra icing sugar. Cut into slices and serve with orange segments, fresh raspberries or a fruit compote.

Variations

✳ You can flavour the cream in the roulade with cooled coffee or melted chocolate, or you can fold through fresh berries, pitted cherries, orange segments or finely chopped preserved stem ginger. You can also add 1–2 tbsp liqueur, to taste, such as Cointreau, Amaretto or Kahlua, before whisking the cream.

STEP 8 Turning the cooled sponge onto a sheet of greaseproof paper dusted with a fine layer of icing sugar.

STEP 9 Spreading the whipped cream filling over the sponge, leaving a 1–2cm clear margin around the edges.

STEP 10 Rolling up the sponge to enclose the filling.

STEP 12 Slicing the roulade to serve.

STRAWBERRY TRIFLE ROULADE

SERVES 6–8

FOR THE SPONGE
Oil, to grease
85g plain flour
Pinch of salt
1 lemon
3 eggs
85g caster sugar, plus
    extra to dust
1½ tbsp warm water

FOR THE FILLING
200g small strawberries

2–3 tbsp Pedro Ximenez
    sherry
1½ tbsp icing sugar, or to
    taste, plus extra to finish
3 tbsp good quality
    strawberry jam
½ quantity crème pâtissière
    (see page 148)

TO SERVE
Strawberry sugar (see note),
    or freeze-dried strawberries

You will need a 30 x 20cm Swiss roll tin or baking tray.

1 To prepare the strawberries for the filling, hull and chop into small pieces. Put in a bowl with the sherry, add the icing sugar and stir gently. Leave to macerate while you make the sponge.

2 Heat the oven to 180°C/gas mark 4. Lightly oil the baking tin and line with baking parchment. Sift the flour and salt onto a sheet of greaseproof paper. Finely grate the lemon zest.

3 Break the eggs into a large heatproof bowl. Add the sugar and lemon zest and, using an electric whisk, start whisking on a low speed without moving the whisk, until combined.

4 Place the bowl over a saucepan of just-boiled water, making sure the base of the bowl is not touching the water, and whisk for 3–4 minutes. Increase the speed and continue whisking until the mixture becomes very fluffy, mousse-like and holds a ribbon for 5–6 minutes (see page 155). Remove the bowl from the pan and continue whisking until the bowl has cooled slightly, a further 2–3 minutes. Lastly, whisk in the water.

5 Sift the flour and salt again over the whisked mixture and fold in carefully, using a large metal spoon or spatula. Spread in the prepared tin, gently smoothing it to the edges. Bake in the middle of the oven for 12–15 minutes until light golden brown and, when lightly pressed, no indentation remains.

6 Remove from the oven and, while still warm, invert the sponge onto a sheet of greaseproof paper sprinkled with caster sugar

and carefully peel off the baking parchment, using a palette knife to support the cake. Trim off the dry edges.

7 Make a shallow cut across the width of the sponge, 1cm in from the edge. Spread the jam over the warm sponge.

8 Transfer the strawberries to a plate, with a slotted spoon. Stir a little of the syrupy juice from the bowl into the crème pâtissière, to taste (but don't make it too thin), then spread over the jam layer. Distribute the strawberries evenly over the crème pâtissière. Using the paper under the sponge to help, roll up the sponge firmly and evenly from the shorter side, enclosing the filling (as shown on page 99). Chill the roulade, wrapped in the paper, to set its shape, for 15–20 minutes.

9 To serve, carefully remove the paper. Dredge the roulade with strawberry sugar or icing sugar and a sprinkling of crushed freeze-dried strawberries. Cut into slices.

To make strawberry sugar...

✱ Blitz a handful of freeze-dried strawberries in a spice grinder to a fine powder, then mix with icing sugar to taste and use as required. Any freeze-dried fruit, such as rhubarb or raspberries, can be used to make fruit sugars, and will last for several weeks in an airtight container. Freeze-dried fruit can be found in large supermarkets or from online food specialist companies.

COCONUT AND MANGO
MERINGUE ROULADE

SERVES 6–8

110g desiccated coconut
3 egg whites
170g caster sugar
½ tsp cornflour
½ tsp white wine vinegar

FOR THE FILLING
1 ripe mango
150ml double cream
2 tbsp icing sugar, plus
    extra to dust

The meringue for a roulade is prepared in the same way as for a Pavlova; the difference is in the cooking. Here the meringue is spread out into a rectangle and cooked until just set, so that it is still flexible once cooled. It is then spread with the filling, rolled up and chilled, then sliced to serve. The filling can, of course, be varied: try sliced strawberries and whipped cream. You will need a 30 x 20cm Swiss roll tin or baking tray.

1 Heat the oven to 180°C/gas mark 4. Line the baking tin with baking parchment, leaving a little excess overhanging the edges of the tin.

2 Spread the coconut out on a baking sheet in a fairly even layer. Toast in the oven for 10–15 minutes, or until the coconut has taken on a light golden colour, stirring it halfway through the cooking time to encourage an even colouring. Remove from the oven and allow to cool completely.

3 In a medium bowl, using an electric whisk, whisk the egg whites to stiff peaks (see page 109). With the beaters still running, whisk in 3 tbsp of the caster sugar, sprinkling 1 tbsp in at a time and whisking the meringue back to stiff peaks again between each addition.

4 Gradually add the remaining sugar in a slow, steady stream, and once it has all been incorporated, continue to whisk only until stiff again. Briefly whisk in the cornflour and vinegar, then fold in half of the toasted coconut, using a large metal spoon or spatula.

5 Pile the meringue into the prepared tin and use a palette knife to spread it evenly into the corners and across the tin. Transfer to the oven and bake for 20–25 minutes until pale golden and lightly springy to the touch. Remove from the oven

and lift the meringue out of the tin by holding the parchment lining and moving it across onto a wire rack. Cover with a few sheets of lightly dampened kitchen paper or a damp tea towel to prevent it from drying out. Leave to cool completely.

6 Meanwhile, for the filling, peel the mango and cut the flesh away from the stone. Purée half in a blender, strain through a sieve and set aside. Cut the remaining mango into 1cm dice.

7 Pour the cream into a medium bowl and add the icing sugar. Whisk until it thickens and just forms soft peaks (see page 72). Fold through the mango purée (do not fold vigorously as it is very easy to over-whip the cream at this stage) and set aside until ready to assemble the roulade.

8 Place a piece of baking parchment on a work surface and sift icing sugar liberally over the surface of the paper. Sprinkle over the remaining coconut and invert the cooled meringue onto the sugared paper (still supported by the wire rack). Carefully peel off the parchment, using a palette knife to support the meringue. Make a shallow cut across the width of the meringue, about 2cm from the edge where you will begin to roll it, which will help to get a well-shaped roll.

9 Spread the mango cream over the meringue, leaving a 2cm clear border around the edge to prevent the cream from spilling out when rolled. Scatter the diced mango over the surface. Start to roll from the cut end, using the paper underneath the meringue to help create a firm and even roll. Don't be alarmed if the meringue has cracked; this is to be expected. Once rolled, refrigerate the roulade wrapped in the paper to set its shape.

10 To serve, transfer to a serving plate and carefully remove the paper. Dust with a little more icing sugar and cut the roulade into slices to serve.

BAKED CHEESECAKE WITH BLACKCURRANT KISSEL

SERVES 8–10

FOR THE BASE
75g butter
150g digestive biscuits
2 tbsp caster sugar

FOR THE TOPPING
6 tbsp caster sugar
20g cornflour
500g cream cheese
2 tsp vanilla extract

4 eggs
200ml double cream

FOR THE KISSEL
450g blackcurrants,
   fresh or frozen
1 orange
1 cinnamon stick
About 170g caster sugar
2 tsp arrowroot

Of Eastern European origin, kissel can be made with any sour soft fruit and served with rice pudding or ice cream, as well as with a baked cheesecake. It can also be made a little thinner and eaten as a sweet soup. As it is served hot, the kissel needs to be thickened at the last minute, but the blackcurrant juice can be made ahead. You will need a 23cm round springform cake tin.

1 Heat the oven to 200°C/gas mark 6. Line the base of the springform tin with greaseproof paper.

2 Melt the butter for the base and crush the biscuits by placing them in a plastic bag and bashing with a rolling pin (or whiz them briefly in a food processor). Transfer to a bowl and stir in the melted butter and the sugar. Press this mixture into the base of the prepared tin. Bake in the oven for 10–15 minutes, then remove and leave to cool.

3 Reduce the oven temperature to 150°C/gas mark 2. For the topping, put 4 tbsp of the sugar with the cornflour into a mixing bowl and, using a wooden spoon, beat in the cream cheese and vanilla.

4 Separate the eggs (see page 56) into 2 medium bowls. Beat the yolks into the cream cheese mixture along with the cream.

5 Whisk the egg whites to medium peaks (see page 109). Whisk in the remaining 2 tbsp sugar, then carefully fold into the cream cheese mixture, using a large metal spoon or spatula.

6 Pour the mixture over the cooled biscuit base and bake in the lower half of the oven for 45–60 minutes until the topping has just set; it should have a slight uniform wobble.

7 Meanwhile, to make the kissel, wash the blackcurrants and remove the stalks, if necessary. Finely grate the orange zest and squeeze the juice. Place the blackcurrants, zest and juice in a medium saucepan with the cinnamon and most of the sugar. Add enough water to come just to the top of the fruit and simmer gently for 20 minutes, or until the fruit is soft.

8 Remove the cinnamon and press the fruit and juice through a sieve, discarding the seeds and skin from the sieve. Return the sieved juices to the pan. Taste and add more sugar if necessary.

9 Once the cheesecake has cooled and is ready to serve, bring the pan of blackcurrant syrup to the boil. Mix the arrowroot with a little cold water in a small bowl to make a smooth paste. Add a ladleful of the hot blackcurrant syrup to the arrowroot and mix thoroughly, then add the arrowroot mixture back into the fruit syrup and stir well. Bring to the boil, stirring, while the mixture thickens. Remove from the heat as soon as it has boiled as, unlike flour, arrowroot should not be simmered.

10 Serve the cheesecake in slices, with some warm kissel poured over each slice.

PEACH MELBA CHEESECAKE

SERVES 8–10

FOR THE BASE
85g unsalted butter
85g digestive biscuits
85g ginger nut biscuits
1 ball of preserved stem
    ginger in syrup, drained

FOR THE FILLING
120g raspberries
2 tbsp icing sugar
150ml crème fraîche
600g cream cheese
55g golden caster sugar

2 tbsp cornflour
3 eggs, plus 2 extra yolks
150ml peach nectar

FOR THE TOPPING
3 ripe peaches
1 tbsp lemon juice
120g raspberries

FOR THE GLAZE
5 tbsp peach jam
    (or apricot if unavailable)
Juice of ½ lemon

Seasonality and quality of ingredients are key here, as you need fragrant, juicy stone fruit and berries that are in their prime. Vary the fruits to reflect the seasons, for example plums in autumn, or figs with pomegranate seeds in winter. Peach nectar is a thick peach juice available from many supermarkets. Alternatively, you can purée 4 or 5 skinned, stoned fresh peaches for the quantity needed and sweeten it to taste with sugar. You will need a 23cm round springform cake tin.

1 Heat the oven to 200°C/gas mark 6.

2 To make the base, melt the butter. Put the biscuits into a strong plastic bag and crush with a rolling pin, or whiz briefly in a food processor and tip into a bowl. Chop the preserved stem ginger finely, add it to the bowl with the melted butter and mix everything together. Press this mixture over the base of the tin and bake in the oven for 10 minutes, then remove and leave to cool. Reduce the oven temperature to 150°C/gas mark 2.

3 Meanwhile, to make the filling, put the raspberries in a small bowl, sprinkle over the icing sugar and set aside. In a separate, large bowl, beat the crème fraîche into the cream cheese with a wooden spoon until the mixture is smooth. Add the sugar, cornflour, eggs and extra yolks and the peach nectar to the creamed mixture and beat well until combined. Crush

the raspberries lightly with the back of a fork, just enough to release some of their juices, but not to break them up, and add them to the cream cheese mixture. Stir them through the mixture quickly and lightly, using a large metal spoon. Do not over-mix; the mixture should have little pockets of raspberries and swirls of marbled raspberry juice running through it.

4 Pour over the biscuit base and bake in the lower half of the oven for 45–60 minutes, or until the filling has just set; there should be a slight uniform wobble. Leave to cool in the tin, then chill in the fridge for at least 2 hours.

5 Meanwhile, to prepare the topping, cut the peaches in half, remove the stones and cut each peach half into 5 or 6 slices. Put the peach slices into a bowl, pour in the lemon juice and stir gently to coat each peach slice.

6 To make the glaze, put the jam and lemon juice in a small saucepan over a low heat and warm until the jam begins to bubble. Strain through a sieve into a small bowl.

7 To assemble, unmould the cheesecake and place on a serving plate. Pat the peach slices dry with kitchen paper and arrange on top. If there are any peach juices left in the bowl, add these to the warm glaze. Arrange the raspberries in the gaps between the peaches. Brush the fruit liberally with the glaze and leave to set for 10–15 minutes. Cut into wedges to serve.

4

MERINGUES

From the crisp meringue discs of the Vacherin to the mallow centred Pavlova, meringue is the perfect accompaniment to fruit and creamy fillings, much loved by adults and children alike. A perfect partner for British soft fruit, the meringue traditionally makes an appearance during the summer months, but swap the berries for chocolate, bottled or poached fruit in season and it becomes a firm year-round favourite.

TYPES AND USES OF MERINGUE

SWISS MERINGUE This is the easiest type of meringue to master and the one most often made at home. It is commonly used for traditional teatime meringues. Egg whites are whisked to stiff peaks (see right), caster sugar is incorporated and the resulting meringue is cooked until it is crisp and dry throughout.

With the addition of a little cornflour and acidity in the form of vinegar or lemon juice, the centre of Swiss meringue will remain soft and mallowy, as in a classic Pavlova. This mallowy centre is perfectly complemented by a topping of fruit and cream.

Swiss meringue can be piped or spooned onto baking sheets lined with baking parchment in a variety of shapes and sizes. Once cooked, it tends to soften quickly on contact with a moist filling, so ideally you should assemble a Swiss meringue pudding no more than half an hour before serving, to keep it crisp. Swiss meringue mixture is not very stable, so make it, shape it and bake it straight away.

ITALIAN MERINGUE A little more complex than Swiss meringue, this is made using granulated sugar in the form of a sugar syrup that is poured over the stiff whisked egg whites, cooking them as the hot syrup is whisked in. Italian meringue is very crisp and dry once baked but, when uncooked, the soft mixture is used in ice cream and mousse recipes to give them airy volume, stability and sweetness. Italian meringue mixture is more stable than Swiss meringue and so can be left for an hour or so before being piped or shaped.

MERINGUE CUITE For this, the liquid whites are whisked with icing sugar over heat, to cook and thicken the egg whites, resulting in a dry and chalky-textured cooked meringue. Meringue cuite mixture is the most stable of all meringues and is the best type for piping into intricate patterns and designs, as it holds its shape well even once cooked. The uncooked meringue is so stable that it can be kept, covered, in the fridge for 24 hours before being piped or shaped and baked.

MAKING MERINGUES

All of the types of meringue described above work by trapping thousands of tiny air bubbles into the egg whites as they are whisked. Whisked egg whites create rather an unstable foam, so to make sure they whisk up well and don't collapse, always use a scrupulously clean bowl to whisk them in.

Traditionally cooks would wipe out a copper bowl with lemon juice and salt to clean the oxidised surface, then the egg whites react with that cleaned copper as they are whisked, producing the best possible volume and stability in the whisked whites. As not many home cooks now have a copper bowl, and whisking by hand with a balloon whisk is exhausting to most of us, we suggest using a clean metal or glass bowl, and a hand-held electric whisk.

China bowls are also fine but plastic bowls tend to trap fat and other impurities in any scratches and it is these that can prevent the egg whites whisking to the necessary stiffness and volume. A stand-alone kitchen mixer is ideal for making meringues, allowing the cook a free hand with which to add sugar, etc.

When making meringues, the ratio of egg whites to sugar is generally 1:2 by weight. So for a meringue made using 100g egg whites you would need 200g sugar. The weights given in our recipes assume you will use medium-sized eggs, where each white will weigh between 25 and 30g (once separated from the yolk and shell).

Unusually, the freshest whites are not the best for making meringues. When the whites have become more of a thick liquid than a gel mass, they break down and trap the air bubbles more easily. So save leftover whites when other recipes require just the yolks and freeze them in small pots labelled with the number of whites they contain. Defrost overnight in the fridge before using them. When using very fresh egg whites, add a pinch of salt to help them break down.

You can now buy cartons of pasteurised egg whites, which means you don't have to find a use for all those leftover yolks when you make meringues. We find they work well, but take a little longer to whisk up than whites from fresh eggs.

TECHNIQUE
WHISKING EGG WHITES

Egg whites must be whisked in clean bowls (see left) just before you need to use them; if left to sit for any length of time they will separate and begin to collapse.

Egg whites are whisked to different extents for different purposes, so it helps to recognise the consistency at the various stages. For meringues, they are whisked until stiff. For most other puddings, egg whites are whisked to a similar texture to the mixture which they are to be combined with.

As you start to whisk the egg whites they will increase in volume, becoming white and foamy. Continue to whisk and the whites will become paler and progressively stiffer, passing through the following recognisable stages.

SOFT PEAK STAGE As the whites are whisked and stiffen, test them by lifting the balloon whisk vertically, then turning the whisk upside down. If the whites cling to the whisk and start to create a 'peak', but the peak falls over on itself, the egg whites have reached the soft peak stage.

MEDIUM PEAK STAGE For firmer whites, whisk for a little longer then test again by lifting the whisk; the whites will cling to the whisk and, as it is pulled up vertically and turned upside down, they will start to fall over onto themselves, then stop halfway. This is the stage used for soufflés and mousses.

STIFF PEAK STAGE Continue to whisk and the whites will become very stiff. When tested the peak will hold its vertical position. This is the stiff peak consistency required for meringue. At this stage there is still some elasticity in the whites. Avoid over-whisking, or they will lose this and break on the whisk.

SHAPING MERINGUES

Meringues should be piped (or spooned) onto baking sheets lined with non-stick baking parchment.

If the meringue is to be piped, put it into a piping bag fitted with a 1–2cm plain or fluted nozzle. Pipe a small dot of meringue onto each corner of the baking sheet before positioning the baking parchment; this will anchor the parchment and make piping easier.

PIPING MERINGUES Using a piping bag fitted with a plain nozzle, pipe 3 squeezes of the bag on top of each other to shape these simple 'beehive' meringues.

INDIVIDUAL VACHERINS Using a piping bag fitted with a plain or fluted nozzle, pipe tight coils of meringue, about 10cm in diameter.

Once cooked, lift the vacherins from the baking parchment. They will be released easily if they are cooked through.

BAKING MERINGUES

Meringues are essentially just a network of bubbles surrounded by sugar and held together with egg whites, so the oven temperature needs to be kept very low, as sugar burns so easily. The normal temperature for cooking meringues of all kinds is between 120°C/gas mark ½ and 140°C/gas mark 1. What also works well is to start meringues cooking in the evening and then turn the oven off and leave them overnight; they will cook and dry out in the residual oven heat. This also applies to Agas or similar ovens – leave meringues in the warming oven overnight to dry and crisp.

To achieve perfectly white meringues, you need to cook them in an electric oven. In a gas oven, meringues – being porous – act as a filter and take on some colour from the gas itself, but this is harmless to eat. If you are using a gas oven, cook meringues on the lowest shelf.

Meringues should be cooked on non-stick baking parchment (or silicone paper) and not greaseproof paper, to which they stick fast when cooked. While greaseproof paper can be lightly greased, this grease can cause the meringue mixture to lose air and collapse and so is not ideal.

To test when meringues are ready, try peeling the baking parchment from the bottom of the meringue; it should come away cleanly and easily.

STORING MERINGUES

When the weather is wet and the air is damp, meringues will absorb moisture and become soft, so wrap them well as soon as they have cooled completely after baking.

Meringues can be made well in advance, which makes them the perfect choice when entertaining for large numbers. Wrapped well in cling film or sealed in an airtight tin or plastic box, they can be made up to a week in advance.

Meringues assembled with sweetened cream can be frozen (although they do lose some crispness), so this is a good use for leftover meringues after a party.

SICILIAN LEMON MERINGUE SUNDAE

SERVES 4

FOR THE MERINGUES
1 Sicilian lemon
2 egg whites
110g caster sugar

FOR THE LEMON CURD
2 Sicilian lemons
85g granulated sugar
40g unsalted butter
2 eggs

FOR THE LIMONCELLO SAUCE AND NEEDLESHREDS
1 Sicilian lemon
150ml double cream
1 tbsp limoncello
1–2 tbsp icing sugar, to taste
100ml water
50g granulated sugar

Sicilian, or Amalfi, lemons are large, juicy and intensely flavoured. They are usually sold unwaxed, with their leaves still attached. If you can't find them, buy regular unwaxed lemons and use a little more zest and juice to achieve the desired sharp, citrus flavour. The meringues, curd and needleshreds can all be made well in advance; the sauce can be made a few hours ahead.

1 For the meringues, heat the oven to 120°C/gas mark ½. Line a baking sheet with baking parchment. Finely grate the zest from the lemon and set aside.

2 In a medium-large bowl, whisk the egg whites to stiff peaks (see page 109), using an electric whisk. With the beaters still running, whisk in the sugar 1 tbsp at a time, whisking the meringue back to stiff peaks again after each addition. Continue until all the sugar has been incorporated. Briefly whisk the lemon zest into the meringue.

3 Drop the meringue mixture in heaped tablespoons onto the baking sheet, leaving a gap between each. Bake in the oven for 1½–2 hours, or until the meringues have dried out completely and will lift off the parchment cleanly. Remove them from the paper and leave to cool completely on a wire rack.

4 Meanwhile, to make the lemon curd, finely grate the zest of the lemons and squeeze the juice. Put the zest and juice in a saucepan with the sugar and butter. Beat the eggs in a bowl to break them up and add them to the pan. Stir over a low heat until the butter and sugar have melted, then increase the heat. Bring the curd just to the boil, stirring continuously, then remove from the heat. Immediately strain through a sieve into a bowl and leave to cool completely; the curd will thicken as it cools. Once cold, cover with cling film and chill until needed.

5 To make the limoncello sauce, finely grate the zest of half of the lemon and pare strips of zest from the other half (see page 11). Squeeze the juice from the whole lemon. Lightly whip the cream in a medium bowl. It should only just hold its shape as it will thicken when it is mixed with the acidic lemon juice.

6 Fold the grated zest and juice into the whipped cream, along with the limoncello and about 1 tbsp sifted icing sugar. Stir together, taste, and add a little more icing sugar if necessary. The sauce should be very tangy and the amount of sugar needed will depend on the size of the lemon and the acidity of the juice. Chill in the fridge until needed.

7 To make the needleshreds, cut the strips of pared zest into very fine strips. Put the water and granulated sugar into a small saucepan. Dissolve the sugar over a low heat, using the handle of a wooden spoon to gently agitate it, then add the zest strips and simmer gently for 10 minutes. Drain and set aside to cool.

8 To assemble, break the meringues into fairly small pieces and place a few pieces in the bottom of each of 4 sundae glasses. Place a little of the lemon curd on top of the meringues, then spoon over a little of the limoncello sauce. Continue layering the ingredients until they are used up, finishing with the limoncello sauce. Decorate with the needleshreds and serve.

SUMMER BERRY PAVLOVA

SERVES 6

FOR THE MERINGUE
4 egg whites
200g caster sugar
1 tsp cornflour
1 tsp vanilla extract
1 tsp white wine vinegar
    or lemon juice

TO ASSEMBLE
300ml double cream
1–2 tbsp icing sugar, to taste
400g mixed soft fruits,
    such as strawberries,
    raspberries, blueberries,
    blackberries and
    redcurrants

This Pavlova can be topped with any combination of lovely summer berries, just be generous! The fruit should liberally cover the cream so that there is enough to balance the sweetness and richness of the creamy meringue.

1 Heat the oven to 140°C/gas mark 1. Line a large baking sheet with non-stick baking parchment.

2 Put the egg whites in a bowl and whisk, using an electric whisk, to stiff peaks (see page 109).

3 Whisk in 4 tbsp of the caster sugar, 1 tbsp at a time, making sure the mixture re-stiffens again after each addition, then fold in the remaining sugar using a large metal spoon. Alternatively, continue whisking while pouring in the remaining sugar in a steady stream.

4 Add the cornflour, vanilla and wine vinegar or lemon juice and whisk briefly, just until incorporated.

5 Pile the meringue in a mound onto the prepared baking sheet and spread out into a circle. (You can draw an 18–20cm diameter circle on the baking parchment to help you, but turn the parchment over before adding the meringue.) Make a shallow dip with the back of a metal spoon in the centre of the meringue mixture to accommodate the cream and fruit.

6 Bake for about 1 hour, or until the shell is firm to the touch and can be peeled off the parchment. Remove from the oven and leave to cool completely.

7 Whisk the cream with the icing sugar in a large bowl until it is just holding its shape. Wash and dry the berries; cut strawberries into halves or quarters if necessary, depending on their size. Pile the cream into the middle of the Pavlova and decorate with the fruit.

Variations

✱ **Golden fruit Pavlova** Top the cream with a mixture of ripe apricot and peach slices, orange segments and even physalis.

✱ **Mango and passion fruit Pavlova** Top the cream with slices cut from 2 or 3 ripe mangoes and the pulp of 4 ripe passion fruit.

✱ **Individual Pavlovas** Make 4–6 individual pavlovas, about 10cm in diameter, and top with sweetened cream and your choice of fruit, as for the main recipe.

Another serving option...

✱ The Pavlova can be inverted before adding the cream and fruit, so the crust stays crisp underneath and the cream sits on the mallowy centre.

VACHERINS WITH SWEET CHESTNUT CREAM

MAKES about 20

FOR THE SWISS MERINGUE
4 egg whites
200g caster sugar

TO ASSEMBLE
350ml double cream
2 tbsp icing sugar
2 tbsp sweetened chestnut
 purée

Made from Swiss meringue, vacherins are tightly piped meringue coils. They take their name from the French cheese Vacherin, which has a similar ridged surface. Sweet chestnut purée is a classic partner for meringue and is sold conveniently in small tins; stir any left over into Greek yoghurt for a delicious quick pudding.

1 Heat the oven to 120°C/gas mark ½. Line 2 baking sheets with non-stick baking parchment. In a medium to large bowl, whisk the egg whites to stiff peaks (see page 109), using an electric whisk.

2 With the beaters still running, whisk in 4 tbsp of the caster sugar, sprinkling 1 tbsp in at a time and whisking the meringue back to stiff peaks again between each addition.

3 Fold in the remaining sugar using a large metal spoon, until just incorporated. Once you are confident with the method, the remaining sugar can be whisked in gradually.

4 Fill a piping bag, fitted with a 5mm–1cm plain or fluted nozzle, with the meringue. Use a little of the meringue to anchor the corners of the baking parchment to the tray.

5 Pipe the meringue mixture into tight 10cm diameter coils (as shown on page 110).

6 Bake in the oven for 1½–2 hours, or until the meringue coils will lift off the parchment cleanly and have fully dried out. Remove from the oven and leave to cool completely.

7 In a large bowl, combine the cream with 1 tbsp of the icing sugar and whisk using a balloon whisk or a hand-held electric whisk until it starts to thicken. Add the chestnut purée and continue to whisk until the mixture just holds its shape. It is very easy to over-whip cream, so take care.

8 Use the chestnut cream to sandwich the meringue coils together. Serve piled on a plate, dusted with the remaining icing sugar.

Variations

✳ **Simple meringues** Make beehive-shaped meringues (see page 110) by piping 3 squeezes of the piping bag on top of each other, each layer smaller than the one before. Omit the chestnut purée from the whipped cream filling. Serve with strawberries, raspberries or other soft fruit.

✳ **Îles flottantes** Whisk 2 tsp cornflour into the meringue mixture after all the sugar has been added, then poach heaped tablespoonfuls of the mixture in a mixture of milk and water for about 2 minutes each side. Serve on a pool of crème anglaise made with half milk and half double cream (see page 146). This can be served drizzled with hot caramel (see page 144).

MACADAMIA MERINGUE CAKE

SERVES 6

FOR THE MERINGUE
150g skinned macadamia
   nuts
300g caster sugar
6 egg whites
2–3 drops of vanilla extract
¾ tsp white wine vinegar

TO ASSEMBLE
300ml double cream
1–2 tbsp icing sugar, to taste,
   plus extra to dust
Melba sauce (see page 149),
   to serve

This is rather a decadent use of macadamia nuts, but well worth it. Once toasted, they impart the most wonderful flavour to this meringue cake. Melba sauce is the ideal fruity complement. You will need two 20cm round cake tins.

1 Heat the oven to 190°C/gas mark 5. Line the cake tins with baking parchment to cover the bottom and sides.

2 Place the macadamia nuts on a baking sheet and roast in the oven for 10–15 minutes, or until lightly browned. Tip onto a plate and set aside to cool.

3 Put the cooled nuts in a blender or food processor with 1 tbsp of the sugar and process until the texture of coarse breadcrumbs. Do not over-process them, or process them while still warm, or they will become greasy.

4 Using an electric whisk, whisk the egg whites in a medium bowl to stiff peaks (see page 109). With the beaters still running, add 4 tbsp caster sugar, sprinkling it in 1 tbsp at a time and making sure the mixture re-stiffens after each addition.

5 Stir the remaining sugar into the ground nuts. Fold the vanilla and wine vinegar into the meringue, then fold in the nuts very carefully, until just combined.

6 Divide the mixture between the tins and level the tops with a palette knife. Bake for about 40 minutes, or until risen a little and light brown.

7 Remove from the oven to a wire rack and leave the meringue rounds to cool completely in the tins. Once cold, carefully remove from the tins, then peel away the baking parchment.

8 Put the cream and icing sugar in a large bowl and whisk until just holding its shape. Sandwich the meringue rounds together with the cream (bottom to bottom) and sift icing sugar over the top. Serve in slices, with the Melba sauce.

Variations

✱ **Hazelnut meringue cake** Replace the macadamia nuts with hazelnuts and proceed as for the main recipe.

✱ **Walnut meringue cake** Replace the hazelnuts with walnuts (the skins are difficult to remove, so leave them on) and proceed as for the main recipe. Stir ½ quantity of lemon curd (see page 112) through the cream to create a marbled effect, before sandwiching the halves together.

RASPBERRY MERINGUE MILLEFEUILLE

SERVES 6–8

FOR THE ITALIAN MERINGUE
200g granulated sugar
100ml water
4 egg whites
½ vanilla pod

FOR THE RASPBERRY PURÉE
200g raspberries
2 tbsp framboise

1 tbsp lemon juice
1 tbsp icing sugar, or to taste

TO ASSEMBLE
150ml double cream
150ml thick crème fraîche
2 tbsp vanilla syrup
1 tbsp icing sugar
350g raspberries
Pink rose petals (optional)
Icing sugar, to dust

This is best assembled shortly before serving. It can also be made with Swiss meringue (see page 116).

1 Heat the oven to 140°C/gas mark 1. Line 2 large baking sheets with non-stick baking parchment. Draw 2 rectangles, 14 x 20cm, on one sheet, with a gap between them to allow for spreading. Draw another rectangle, the same size, on the other sheet, so you have 3 templates. Turn the parchment over.

2 To make the meringue, put the sugar and water into a small, heavy-based saucepan. Dissolve over a very low heat, stirring gently without splashing up the sides of the pan. When the sugar has dissolved, brush down the sides of the pan with a pastry brush dipped in water, then increase the heat. Do not stir the syrup once the sugar has dissolved. Using a sugar thermometer to check, boil the syrup until it reaches 120°C.

3 Meanwhile, using an electric whisk, whisk the egg whites in a medium bowl to stiff peaks (see page 109). As soon as the syrup reaches 120°C, pour it steadily onto the egg whites with the beaters running. Try not to pour it onto the actual beaters as the syrup can solidify on them. Continue whisking until the mixture is cool and stiff. Split the half vanilla pod lengthways, scrape out the seeds and whisk them into the meringue.

4 Set aside a generous third of the meringue. Divide the rest equally between 2 templates. Using a palette knife, spread the meringue in a thin, even layer, smoothing it right to the edges. These 2 thin sheets will form the base and middle layers of

the millefeuille. Spread the remaining meringue over the third template to the edges, then use the back of a teaspoon to swirl the meringue into little peaks; this will form the top layer.

5 Bake the meringues in the lower third of the oven for 45–50 minutes, or until they will lift off the parchment cleanly and have completely dried out. Remove from the oven and leave to cool completely. The top layer of meringue may need to cook for a little longer than the 2 plain layers, as it is thicker.

6 Meanwhile, for the purée, put the raspberries, framboise, lemon juice and icing sugar in a small pan over a low heat and bring slowly to the boil. Press through a sieve, to remove the seeds, into a clean pan. Return to the heat. Boil for 1 minute, or until reduced by about half; it should be an intensely flavoured fairly thick purée. Transfer to a small bowl and chill until needed.

7 To make the filling, whip the cream to soft peaks (see page 72) in a medium bowl. Stir in the crème fraîche, vanilla syrup and icing sugar. Chill until needed.

8 To assemble the millefeuille, place a plain sheet of meringue on a serving platter and carefully spread half of the cream mixture over it. Drizzle half of the raspberry purée over the cream and top with a third of the raspberries. Place a second sheet of meringue on top and repeat the cream, purée and fruit layers. Top with the thicker, swirled sheet of meringue.

9 Decorate with the remaining raspberries and the rose petals, if using. Dust with icing sugar and serve, cut into slices.

PISTACHIO PAVLOVA WITH ORANGES AND POMEGRANATE

SERVES 8

FOR THE MERINGUE
125g shelled unsalted
   pistachios
200g caster sugar
4 egg whites
1 tsp cornflour
2 tsp orange blossom water
1 tsp white wine vinegar or
   lemon juice

TO ASSEMBLE
4 oranges (blood oranges,
   if in season)
1 pomegranate
200ml double cream
200g mascarpone
2 tbsp runny honey

This colourful Pavlova is also lovely made as individual desserts – single portion sized Pavlovas will cook in about 45 minutes. You could also sprinkle on some rose petals to add to the Middle Eastern theme.

1 Heat the oven to 140°C/gas mark 1. Line a baking sheet with non-stick baking parchment.

2 Put 100g of the pistachios into the small bowl of a food processor or coffee grinder with 1 tbsp of the sugar and process until the texture of coarse breadcrumbs. Do not over-process or the nuts will become greasy.

3 Using an electric whisk, whisk the egg whites in a medium bowl to stiff peaks (see page 109). With the beaters still running, add 4 tbsp of the sugar, sprinkling in 1 tbsp at a time and whisking the mixture back to stiff peak after each addition.

4 Fold the remaining sugar into the ground nuts along with the cornflour. Fold the orange blossom water and vinegar into the meringue, then fold in the nuts and sugar very carefully, until just combined.

5 Pile the meringue into a mound on the prepared baking sheet and spread it out into a circle. (You can draw an 18–20cm diameter circle on the baking parchment to help you, turning the parchment over before covering with the meringue if you like.) Make a shallow dip with the back of a metal spoon in the centre of the meringue mixture (to accommodate the cream and fruit).

6 Bake in the oven for 1–1¼ hours, or until the shell is firm to the touch and the parchment can be peeled away from the meringue. Remove from the oven and leave to cool completely.

7 Segment the oranges (see page 10). To remove the seeds from the pomegranate, roll it on the work surface to loosen the seeds, cut it in half and bash the rounded end with a wooden spoon over a bowl to catch the seeds.

8 Mix the cream, mascarpone and honey in a large bowl and whisk until the mixture is just holding its shape. Pile into the middle of the Pavlova and decorate with the orange segments, pomegranate seeds and remaining pistachios.

5

ICE CREAMS
AND SORBETS

Ice creams and sorbets are often served as an accompaniment
to another dessert that is really the main event. However,
many of these recipes can happily take centre stage as the
perfect way to showcase the best of fruit in season, or to
enjoy a rich, sweet treat. There are a wide variety of fruit
salads and compotes in the first chapter (see pages 12–25)
that make perfect partners to some of these ice creams.
For extra texture, add a sprinkling of praline (see page 132)
or serve a crisp tuile (see page 150) on the side.

MAKING
ICES AND SORBETS

ICE CREAM MAKING METHODS

Ice creams can be made in several different ways. The most common method is a custard-based ice cream where a crème anglaise (or custard) base is flavoured, then churned to break up rocky ice crystals as it freezes, and to introduce some air which will make the ice cream smooth, creamy and light.

Meringue-based and mousse-based ice creams are made by folding lightly whipped cream and all manner of flavourings into Italian meringue or a mousse base. In both methods, air bubbles are introduced when making the base, resulting in a light textured ice cream. Sometimes these ice creams don't need to be churned, as so much air is already incorporated. A parfait is just such an un-churned ice cream, light because of all the air whisked into it.

As the name suggests, an all-in-one ice cream is made with a creamy mixture that is churned without having to make a custard, mousse or meringue base first. They are very simple to make but must have quite a high fat content to achieve a similarly creamy texture to the alternative ice cream methods. The all-in-one method is often used for frozen yoghurts.

SORBETS AND GRANITAS

Sorbets are the most widely made water ice, and are made by churning and freezing a flavoured syrup or fruit purée so that the ice crystals become very small and the sorbet feels smooth on the tongue as you eat it. Sometimes liquid glucose is added too, which helps to keep the sorbet soft and smooth, as well as stabilising the sugar syrup.

Granitas are made with slightly less sugar and are not churned or blended. They have an even texture of coarse crystals which are created by forking or breaking up the mixture several times during the freezing process.

CHURNING AND FREEZING

Churning gives a smooth ice cream or sorbet by breaking down the crystals, and it also incorporates some air into the mixture, which gives the ice a lightness.

If an ice cream or sorbet mixture is frozen without being churned, the water in the mixture freezes into large crystals

which makes it appear rocky, rough and heavy when eaten. It also makes the ice cream or sorbet difficult to scoop. There are several ways to prevent this happening and give a smooth, scoopable texture.

Churning means stirring or blending the mixture as it freezes to break down large, crunchy ice crystals into tiny ones, giving a smooth texture. The easiest way to do this is by using an ice-cream machine. There are many different models to choose from. Some simply plug in and freeze your mixture while a paddle stirs continuously and breaks down the crystals as they form. Some machines require the bowl to be frozen and then an electric paddle is fitted into it, and some even require you to turn a handle by hand.

If you plan to buy a machine that does not freeze the ice cream itself, check that you have room in your freezer to accommodate the bowl, which may be quite bulky. They vary greatly in price and can deal with different volumes of ice cream, but all should be able to produce a well textured ice cream.

If you don't have an ice-cream machine, you can still make a delicious ice cream or sorbet, it just takes a little more effort. Freeze the mixture in a shallow container until it is half frozen, so you can still press a teaspoon into the mixture although it is no longer liquid. If you have a food processor, turn out the half frozen mixture onto a board, cut it into chunks with a large knife, and pulse it quickly in the processor, in batches, without allowing the mixture to melt completely, then return it immediately to the container and the freezer. Allow the ice to freeze again then repeat this once or twice more for a really smooth textured result.

If you do not have a food processor, freeze the mixture in a shallow container until large crystals start to form around the outside of the container but there is still some liquid in the middle. Remove the container from the freezer and whisk vigorously with a balloon whisk, without allowing the mixture to melt completely, then return to the freezer. Repeat this process 2 or 3 more times. The result will not be as smooth as using an ice-cream machine or food processor.

Ice cream and sorbet texture

ACHIEVING A GOOD TEXTURE

There are other factors besides churning which affect the texture and set of an ice cream or sorbet. By set, we mean how firm it is when it has been frozen. Ideally it will freeze almost hard but have softened sufficiently to scoop easily if transferred from the freezer to the fridge about 20–30 minutes before serving. If it is too soft, it will melt before it can be scooped and served.

SUGAR

All sweet ice creams and sorbets need sugar, both for seasoning and to soften the set. Sugar prevents the ice cream or sorbet from freezing completely solid, thus making it soft enough to scoop. However, too much sugar can prevent it freezing at all. Taste the mixture while you are making it when it is at room temperature, but be aware that when it has frozen, it will taste less sweet, so be generous with the sweetening. If you make an ice cream or sorbet that won't set however long it is frozen and churned, taste it to see if it is over-sweet. If it is, it will need to be diluted with water or another liquid from the recipe before it will freeze.

ALCOHOL

A little alcohol adds a punch of flavour, but, like sugar, prevents the water in the ice from freezing solid, and too much alcohol prevents it from freezing at all. Unless it is heated to a high temperature and for a long period during the cooking process (which would drive off the alcohol), the alcohol is still present and can interfere with the ice freezing.

FAT

Fat is generally present in ice creams and not in water ices like sorbets, although some sorbets do have a little, such as the buttermilk sorbet on page 137. Fat in the form of cream, crème fraîche or even Greek yoghurt, helps to produce a rich smooth texture, but if the fat content is too high, the texture becomes unpleasant and almost chalky, and it will crumble when you try to scoop it.

EGGS

Egg yolks add a creamy texture to ice creams, while egg whites give a smooth silky texture to sorbets. Make sure if you are feeding vulnerable groups, such as pregnant women or the elderly, to use pasteurised yolks or whites, now available from many supermarkets as well as specialist shops.

Serving ice creams and sorbets

Although ice creams and sorbets can be stored in a freezer for up to 3 months and still be eaten safely, they are best eaten less than 24 hours after making, as this is when the texture and flavour will be at their best.

Transfer the ice cream or sorbet from the freezer to the fridge 20–30 minutes before you want to serve it to allow it to soften a little, making it easier to scoop.

If you are serving balls of ice cream to a number of people, it is a good idea to prepare them in advance, thus removing the stress of scooping while everyone is waiting to eat. Cover a metal tray in cling film and chill in the freezer for at least 30 minutes. Meanwhile, remove the ice cream or sorbet from the freezer and leave it out for 20 minutes to soften a little. Scoop the ice cream into balls, placing them on the chilled tray as you make them. Return the tray to the freezer as soon as possible to prevent the ice cream balls from melting. When you are ready to serve, simply remove the tray from the freezer and place a ball of ice cream or sorbet on each plate.

A useful tip is to sift a little icing sugar onto each plate to stop a ball of ice cream slipping around.

VANILLA ICE CREAM

SERVES 4

200ml whole milk	4 egg yolks
200ml double cream	75g caster sugar
1 vanilla pod	Pinch of salt

This classic ice cream is made from crème anglaise. It is the basic method for a whole variety of custard based ice creams as you can see from the numerous variations. Leaving the vanilla pod in the custard while it cools completely is really important to infuse the maximum vanilla flavour into the ice cream itself.

1 Put the milk and cream into a saucepan. Split the vanilla pod in half lengthways and add it to the pan. Bring to scalding point (see page 155), then remove from the heat and set aside for 20 minutes to allow the vanilla flavour to infuse.

2 Put the yolks in a bowl with the sugar and salt, and mix well. Pour in the cream mixture and stir well. Return the mixture to the rinsed out pan and cook over a low to medium heat, stirring constantly, until the custard coats the back of the wooden spoon (see page 146); do not allow it to boil.

3 Strain the custard into a bowl. Scrape the seeds from the vanilla pod into the custard. Leave to cool completely.

4 Churn the mixture in an ice-cream machine, then transfer to a plastic container and put into the freezer until needed. Alternatively, freeze the mixture in a shallow tray. When it is just frozen, cut into chunks and briefly whiz it in a food processor, then immediately return to the freezer. Repeat this process when it has just re-frozen to create a smooth-textured ice cream. After the second whizzing, transfer the ice cream to a plastic container.

5 Transfer the tub of ice cream from the freezer to the fridge 20–30 minutes before serving to soften slightly before serving, scooped into glass bowls.

Variations

✱ **Coffee ice cream** Omit the vanilla and add 5 tsp instant coffee granules to the milk and cream before scalding; this gives a good intense flavour. Alternatively, you can also replace some of the liquid measurement with coffee essence or 6 shots of espresso.

✱ **Cinnamon ice cream** Omit the vanilla, break a cinnamon stick into 3 pieces and add to the milk and cream before scalding. Leave to infuse for at least 30 minutes then proceed as for the main recipe.

✱ **Chocolate malt ice cream** Omit the vanilla. Add 100g good quality dark chocolate, cut into pieces, 2 tbsp malt extract and ½ tsp vanilla extract to the milk and cream. Bring to scalding point, stirring to melt the chocolate, then proceed as for the main recipe.

✱ **Coconut ice cream** Use 300ml coconut milk and 100ml double cream or coconut cream. Omit the vanilla and proceed as for the main recipe.

✱ **Salted caramel ice cream** Omit the vanilla and add ¼ tsp Maldon salt flakes to the milk and cream before scalding. Make a dry caramel with the sugar (see page 144), taking it to a deep golden colour. Slowly and carefully (it will splutter) pour the scalded milk and cream onto the caramel to stop it cooking, and reheat gently to ensure all the caramel is dissolved. Add this to the egg yolks and stir well, then proceed as for the main recipe.

✱ **Christmas cake and Madeira ice cream** Roughly crumble 200g rich fruit cake into a bowl, pour on 5 tbsp Madeira and leave to soak for 20–30 minutes. Make the ice cream as for the main recipe, omitting the milk and using 600ml double cream, 1 vanilla pod and 5 egg yolks. Once the ice cream is churned until thick, transfer to a bowl and stir in the crumbled fruit cake and any Madeira left in the bowl. Freeze and serve as above.

CLOTTED CREAM RASPBERRY RIPPLE ICE CREAM

SERVES 6

350g raspberries
250g caster sugar
100ml water
1 tbsp lemon juice

4 egg whites
Few drops of vanilla extract
100g clotted cream
100ml double cream

This meringue based ice cream doesn't require an ice cream machine for churning as so much air is incorporated into the egg whites. It is equally delicious made with a purée of blackcurrants. You will need a 450g loaf tin or mould, lined with cling film.

1 Put the raspberries in a saucepan with 100g of the sugar. Cover with a lid and cook gently over a low to medium heat until the raspberries are completely soft, stirring occasionally.

2 Press the raspberries through a sieve, trying to push as much of the pulp through as possible; you should have about 250g raspberry purée.

3 Put the remaining 150g sugar into another saucepan, with the water and lemon juice. Dissolve over a low heat, moving the sugar over the bottom of the pan very gently without stirring or allowing it to splash up the sides of the pan. Once dissolved, increase the heat and boil the syrup until it registers 120°C on a sugar thermometer, i.e. the firm ball stage, when a small piece, cooled in water, will form a firm but not hard ball between the fingers (see page 142).

4 Meanwhile, as the syrup reaches 110°C, begin to whisk the egg whites to stiff peaks (see page 109), using an electric whisk. As soon as the syrup has reached 120°C, pour it onto the egg whites, with the beaters still running, taking care not to pour the syrup onto the beaters or it may set hard on the metal.

5 Continue to whisk until the mixture becomes a stiff meringue. Stir the vanilla into the clotted cream to loosen it. Lightly whip the double cream to very soft peaks (see page 72), then fold in the clotted cream.

6 Fold the cream mixture into the meringue. Add the raspberry purée and, using a metal spoon, marble it into the ice cream with as few stirs as possible.

7 Carefully pour the mixture into the prepared tin or mould, and freeze overnight, or for at least several hours.

8 Transfer the ice cream from the freezer to the fridge 20–30 minutes before serving, to allow it to soften slightly. Slice or scoop to serve.

POPCORN ICE CREAM
WITH POPCORN BRITTLE

SERVES 4

FOR THE POPCORN
75ml sunflower oil
75g popping corn

FOR THE ICE CREAM
200ml whole milk
200ml double cream
5 egg yolks
75g caster sugar

Pinch of salt
30g unsalted butter

FOR THE BRITTLE
Oil, to grease
80g granulated sugar
60ml water
20g salted butter, chilled

Popcorn makes an unusual and delicious ice cream flavour – a treat for the whole family. If you do not have a very large saucepan with a lid, make the popcorn in 2 batches.

1 First make the popcorn. Heat the oil in a very large saucepan over a medium heat. Add a few kernels of corn and put the lid on the pan. When the corn begins to pop, add the rest of the kernels and return the lid immediately. When the last of the added corn kernels begin to pop, turn the heat down a little and shake the pan occasionally to evenly distribute the heat. Leave the lid on until the corn finishes popping, then remove from the heat.

2 For the ice cream, put the milk, cream and half the popcorn into a large saucepan. Bring to scalding point (see page 155), then remove from the heat and leave to infuse for 2 hours.

3 Pass the mixture through a fine sieve into a bowl, using a ladle to help push it through. Discard the squeezed out popcorn, return the infused milk and cream to the pan and bring to a simmer.

4 Meanwhile, put the egg yolks in a bowl with the sugar and salt, and mix well. Pour in the hot infused milk and cream and stir well. Return the mixture to the rinsed out pan and cook over a low to medium heat, stirring constantly, until the custard thickens enough to coat the back of a wooden spoon (see page 146); do not allow it to boil.

5 Once thickened, immediately strain the custard through a sieve into a bowl and whisk in the butter. Leave to cool.

6 Once cooled, churn the mixture in an ice-cream machine (or, if you do not have one, follow the instructions on page 124), then transfer to a plastic container and freeze overnight.

7 To make the brittle, lightly oil a large baking sheet. Put the sugar and water into a medium pan and dissolve over a low heat. When all the sugar has dissolved, brush down the sides of the pan using a wet pastry brush (as shown on page 143) and turn up the heat until the syrup is bubbling. Cook without stirring until it turns a deep golden caramel. Remove from the heat and immediately whisk in the butter.

8 Add the remaining popcorn, quickly stir to coat it evenly in the caramel and tip the mixture out onto the oiled tray, in a fairly even layer. Leave to cool and harden.

9 Transfer the ice cream from the freezer to the fridge 20–30 minutes before serving, to soften slightly, before scooping into a cold bowl. Break up the popcorn brittle and scatter over the ice cream to serve. Any extra brittle can be stored in an airtight container for up to a week, although it is unlikely that it will last that long…

PRALINE PARFAIT

110g skinned hazelnuts
Oil, to grease
280g caster sugar

500ml double cream
6 egg whites

This is the frozen dessert to make if you don't have an ice-cream machine, as it doesn't require churning. It can be frozen in any individual ramekins or moulds lined with cling film, or in a lined loaf tin and then sliced to serve; or, as the recipe suggests, it can simply be frozen ready to scoop.

1 Heat the oven to 180°C/gas mark 4. Spread the hazelnuts out on a baking sheet and roast for 10–15 minutes, or until they have an even golden colour, then remove from the oven. Lightly oil a second baking sheet.

2 Sprinkle 110g of the sugar evenly over the surface of a large frying pan; ideally the sugar should be no thicker than 2–3mm to ensure quick and even melting and colouring. Place the pan over a low heat. The sugar will start to melt at the edges, but do not be tempted to stir it. As more sugar melts and takes on colour, carefully swirl the pan to encourage even browning. You may need to use a wooden spoon or heatproof spatula to redistribute the unmelted sugar to the outside of the pan.

3 When all the sugar has melted, continue to cook until the caramel has taken on a deep golden colour, then immediately take off the heat and carefully add the still warm nuts. Stir to coat the nuts in the caramel evenly, then quickly turn the praline mixture out onto the oiled baking sheet. Set aside and allow to cool completely.

4 Pour the cream into a bowl and whip until thickened and just starting to form soft peaks (see page 72). Set aside in the fridge until needed.

5 When the praline is cool, place it in a strong plastic bag, ensure the bag is sealed and, using a rolling pin or small saucepan, gently bash to break it up into small pieces no larger than the size of a hazelnut.

6 In a large, very clean bowl, whisk the egg whites until they form stiff peaks (see page 109). With the beaters still running, whisk in 6 tbsp of the remaining sugar, sprinkling in 1 tbsp at a time and whisking the meringue back to stiff peaks again between each addition. Gradually whisk in the remaining sugar until it is all incorporated and the meringue has returned to stiff peaks.

7 Fold the whipped cream and crushed praline gently into the egg whites, using a large metal spoon or a spatula until the mixture is evenly combined. Transfer to a plastic container, cover and freeze well before use.

8 Transfer the parfait to the fridge 20–30 minutes before serving, to soften enough to scoop.

PASSION FRUIT PARFAIT

SERVES 6–8

150g granulated sugar
75ml water
5 egg yolks
300ml double cream
250ml passion fruit juice

FOR THE ITALIAN MERINGUE
150g granulated sugar
75ml water
2 egg whites

This parfait can be set in glasses, individual dishes or even on a layer of cake or biscuit base.

1 For the mousse base, put the sugar and water into a medium saucepan over a low heat, to slowly dissolve the sugar. You can gently move the sugar on the base of the pan with the handle of a wooden spoon to prevent it caking on the bottom of the pan (as shown on 143) but don't allow it to splash up the sides.

2 Once the sugar has dissolved, brush down the sides of the pan using a pastry brush dipped in water (see page 143). Turn up the heat and, without stirring, boil the syrup until it registers 120°C on a sugar thermometer, i.e. the firm ball stage, when a small piece, cooled in water, will form a firm but not hard ball between the fingers (see page 142).

3 Put the egg yolks into a heatproof bowl and, when the sugar syrup reaches 110°C, start whisking the yolks using a hand-held electric whisk, until pale.

4 Once the syrup reaches 120°C, pour it in a steady drizzle onto the yolks while whisking continuously, then carry on whisking until the mixture is cool, pale, thick and mousse-like. Set aside until needed.

5 To make the Italian meringue, put the sugar and water into a medium saucepan and slowly dissolve the sugar following the instructions in step 1, then increase the heat and boil until the syrup reaches 120°C on a sugar thermometer. Meanwhile, put the egg whites into a heatproof bowl and, when the sugar syrup reaches 110°C, start whisking them to stiff peaks (see page 109).

6 Once the syrup reaches the necessary temperature, pour it in a steady drizzle over the egg whites, whisking until cool.

7 Lightly whip the cream until it is just holding its shape.

8 Pour the passion fruit juice around the edge of the egg yolk mousse and fold it through, using a spatula, until incorporated.

9 Fold in half of the whipped cream, followed by half of the Italian meringue and then repeat until all 3 mixtures are just combined. Be careful not to knock out all the air by over-folding.

10 Pour the parfait into glasses, moulds or pastry cutters lined with cling film and place in the freezer. Transfer to the fridge 20 minutes before serving, to soften slightly.

BLOOD ORANGE SORBET WITH ICED VODKA

SERVES 6–8

1 litre blood orange juice
320g caster sugar
1 tbsp liquid glucose

90–120ml freezer-chilled
vodka (optional)

Make this sorbet using a carton of freshly squeezed blood orange juice, or the juice from fresh blood oranges if they are in season. Each blood orange will yield around 60ml juice, so you will need about 16 of them. Liquid glucose is used to make the syrup stable and less likely to crystallise, and also to help give the sorbet its smooth texture. Serve the sorbet with blood orange segments in place of the vodka if children will be eating it.

1 Put half of the blood orange juice in a medium saucepan with the sugar and liquid glucose. Slowly heat over a low to medium heat until the sugar has completely dissolved.

2 Remove the pan from the heat and pour in the remaining juice, stir well and leave the mixture to cool.

3 When cold, transfer to an ice-cream machine and churn until semi-frozen and thick (or see page 124). Transfer the churned sorbet to a plastic container, cover and freeze overnight.

4 Transfer the orange sorbet from the freezer to the fridge 20–30 minutes before scooping and serving. Scoop the sorbet into chilled serving dishes and top with 1 tbsp ice-cold vodka, if using. Serve immediately.

WHITE PEACH SORBET

SERVES 6–8

300g granulated sugar
300ml water
45g liquid glucose

500g white peach purée
   (Funkin Pro or Boiron)
1 lemon

This sorbet is extremely quick and easy to make, especially if you are using the high quality peach purées available through specialist shops and online. Of course, you could also make your own using perfectly ripe white peaches, available for a very short season, or the more common golden peaches.

1 Put the sugar, water and liquid glucose into a saucepan and heat until the sugar has dissolved, stirring occasionally. Bring to the boil and simmer until the syrup registers 108°C on a sugar thermometer; i.e. the short thread stage – when a small piece will form a thread that extends to 5–7mm between the fingers (see page 142).

2 Immediately pour in the white peach purée, stir and allow the mixture to cool slightly. Juice the lemon and add enough lemon juice to taste, starting with 1 tbsp.

3 Once completely cool, churn the sorbet in an ice-cream machine (or see page 124) and then spoon it into a container and freeze until firm.

4 Transfer the peach sorbet from the freezer to the fridge 20–30 minutes before scooping and serving.

A note on using fresh peaches...

✱ You will need about 8 very ripe medium peaches to make the 500g purée needed for this recipe. Skin, halve and stone the peaches, then purée in a blender until smooth and sweeten to taste with caster sugar. Push the purée through a sieve to make it really smooth.

BUTTERMILK SORBET

SERVES 6–8

110ml water
110g granulated sugar
1 lemon

½ vanilla pod
480ml buttermilk

This simple but delicious sorbet has a delicate flavour that works really well served with fruit. Try it with hot crumbles or cobblers or with summer berry compote for a light summer pudding. The syrup used to make the sorbet could also be infused with herbs such as thyme or basil for a really interesting and subtle flavour. Simply strain out the herbs before adding the chilled syrup to the buttermilk mixture.

1 Pour the water into a small saucepan, stir in the sugar and slowly bring to a simmer, occasionally stirring gently until the sugar has dissolved, but without splashing the syrup up the sides of the saucepan. Remove from the heat, allow to cool, then chill until needed.

2 Finely grate the lemon zest and squeeze the juice. Scrape out the seeds from the half vanilla pod. In a large bowl, whisk together the buttermilk, sugar syrup, vanilla seeds and the lemon juice and zest.

3 Churn the mixture in an ice-cream machine (or see page 124), then spoon into a plastic container, remembering to remove it from the freezer to the fridge 20–30 minutes before you want to scoop it.

STRAWBERRY GRANITA

SERVES 4

½–1 tsp coarsely ground
    black pepper
150g granulated sugar

600ml water
1 lemon
350g fresh strawberries

This is an incredibly refreshing dessert, with an intense strawberry flavour, best served in glasses without delay – to enjoy the crumbly icy crystals on a summer's day. Strong or sharp flavours work best with the large icy crystals of a granita, so the coffee variation is very good too.

1 Put the pepper, sugar and water in a heavy-based saucepan over a low to medium heat to dissolve the sugar. Once the sugar has dissolved, increase the heat and simmer for 4–5 minutes, or until the syrup registers 104°C on a sugar thermometer and has a slightly greasy, sticky feel of 'vaseline' when a small piece is held between the fingers (see page 142).

2 Remove from the heat and set aside to cool. Juice the lemon.

3 Blend the strawberries until smooth in a food processor or mash them to a purée, then push them through a sieve to remove the seeds.

4 Once the syrup is cool, strain it into the purée, add the lemon juice to taste and stir well.

5 Place the mixture in a shallow container and freeze for about 1–2 hours, or until beginning to solidify at the edges.

6 Remove from the freezer and stir with a fork to mix the ice crystals evenly. Return it to the freezer until the granita is again beginning to solidify at the edges.

7 Repeat this stirring process 2 or 3 times, or until the granita has an even texture of small ice crystals; it should be grainy but not mushy. Serve immediately.

Variation

✱ Coffee granita Put 6 shots of strong espresso coffee in a measuring jug and make up to 600ml with water. Pour the coffee into a saucepan, add 120g granulated sugar and dissolve over a low to medium heat, then set aside to cool. Once the syrup is cool, add 1–2 tbsp Kahlua, Tia Maria or other coffee liqueur, to taste. Freeze, stirring at intervals, as for the above granita.

A note on preparing ahead...

✱ If you want to prepare the granita a day in advance, remove it from the freezer 2 hours before serving and leave to soften for 30 minutes. Stir thoroughly with a fork, then return to the freezer. After a further 30 minutes, stir once more and refreeze until ready to serve.

6

SAUCES AND DESSERT BISCUITS

Here are the finishing touches that will elevate a simple pudding to an elegant dessert. A shard of crisp caramel or an almond tuile will transform a ball of ice cream, and a Calvados crème anglaise will turn a classic apple crumble from family weekday favourite to a signature pudding. The dessert biscuits can all be prepared a few days ahead so do make a batch if you are entertaining.

STOCK SYRUP

MAKES about 500ml

250g granulated sugar
500ml water

. . . .

This basic syrup can be made in a large quantity and kept in the fridge for general purpose use, such as making coulis or macerating fruit.

1 Put the sugar and water in a medium saucepan. Place over a low heat to dissolve the sugar, using the handle of a wooden spoon to gently agitate it and prevent it from 'caking' on the bottom of the pan. Avoid splashing syrup up the sides.

2 Once the sugar has dissolved, use a pastry brush dipped in water to brush down the sides of the pan, to wash any remaining sugar crystals down into the syrup.

3 Turn the heat up and do not stir from this point. Bring the syrup to the boil and boil steadily for 5 minutes. Take off the heat, leave to cool and keep covered until needed.

. . . .

A note on crystallisation...

Sugar crystals attract each other. If a few crystals are still present after the sugar has dissolved, when the syrup is boiled these crystals may contaminate the syrup and turn the dissolved sugar into crystals again, crystallising the entire sugar syrup. If this happens you will need to discard the mixture and start again with fresh ingredients.

A sound technique will prevent crystallisation. However, when sugar syrups are to be used for very sensitive recipes, then an interfering agent can be added to the syrup when dissolving the sugar. Interfering agents include glucose syrup or some form of acidity such as a few drops of lemon juice or a pinch of cream of tartar. These invert the sugar (sucrose), breaking it down into different sugars (glucose and fructose), which makes the mixture more stable and helps to prevent crystallisation.

Stages in sugar syrup concentration

When you are ready to use the syrup, bring it to the boil in a saucepan and boil for the length of time necessary for it to reach the correct temperature and required consistency. This will depend on what the syrup will be used for, ranging from 104–108°C for sugar syrup and sorbets to 194°C for a deep golden caramel.

Up to the 'soft ball' stage (115°C), you can test the consistency by using a teaspoon and your fingers, but take care as the syrup will be hot. Draw the pan off the heat, dip the teaspoon in and take a little of the syrup between the thumb and forefinger and test it (as shown).

Above this temperature the syrup will be too hot to use your fingers, so take a little of it with a teaspoon, drop into a jug of cold water, let cool, then take out and feel it.

. . . .

Taking a syrup too far...

If a syrup is taken to a stage too far, it can be brought back by the addition of a good splash of water so the sugar density is diluted again. This can only be done if the syrup has not yet taken on colour. Once colour is achieved, the caramel can be stopped, but there is no going back to a previous stage.

. . . .

A note on safety...

Take care when making and using sugar syrups as the temperature of the syrup goes well above 100°C.

1 Agitating the sugar to stop it caking.

2 Brushing down any sugar crystals.

3 Boiling the sugar syrup.

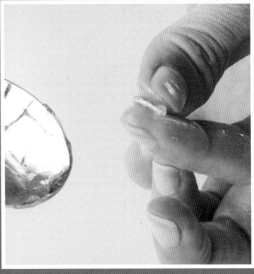

TESTING THE BOILING STAGE Checking the consistency of the sugar syrup between the thumb and forefinger.

CARAMEL

MAKES about 450g

A little oil
500g granulated sugar

250ml water

This will produce a brittle caramel that can either be broken into shards or drizzled onto an oiled baking sheet to harden and used for decoration.

1 Very lightly oil a baking tray. Put the sugar and water into a heavy-based saucepan. Place over a low heat and dissolve the sugar, using the handle of a wooden spoon to gently agitate the sugar to prevent it from 'caking' on the bottom of the saucepan (as shown on page 143). Try to avoid splashing syrup up the sides of the pan.

2 Brush down the sides of the pan with a pastry brush dipped in water to remove any sugar crystals (as shown on page 143), then bring the syrup to a gentle boil. Boil the syrup, without stirring, until it is an even, rich golden colour. It may be necessary to swirl the caramel to encourage even colouring.

3 Pour the caramel onto the oiled baking tray or quickly drizzle a pattern using a spoon. Wait for the caramel to cool completely and set before releasing it from the baking sheet and breaking it into pieces. It should be used soon after it is made as it will soon become sticky.

Controlling the cooking and colour of caramel...

Making a caramel requires confidence and decisive action. As the sugar syrup begins to take on colour, turn the heat down a little to slow the caramelisation of the sugar and give you more control of the cooking. Don't leave it; sugar burns very quickly. As the sugar starts to caramelise you may need to give the saucepan a gentle swirl to ensure the sugar caramelises evenly.

As the sugar colours more it will begin to smoke lightly. Watch the caramel carefully. Take the pan off the heat and swirl the caramel gently; this will help to reduce the size of the bubbles and allow you to see its true colour. If it is not the colour you require then return the pan to the heat and continue cooking.

When the caramel reaches a rich golden colour, it is ready and you must act quickly to take it off the heat and pour it out of the pan. Even off the heat the caramel will continue to deepen in colour, and too deep a colour will cause bitterness.

If you want to use the caramel to make a sauce, add water or cream to it to stop the cooking. It is best to have any liquid to hand and ready to use when you need it. The water needs to be poured onto the caramel when you think it is just a shade less than the desired colour, as the heat in the caramel will continue to colour it in the few seconds it takes to lift the liquid and pour it in. Stand well back when adding liquid to caramel, as it will splutter and spit alarmingly at first.

Making a dry caramel...

It is possible to make a caramel without water. It is slightly quicker as the sugar does not need dissolving and the water does not need to be evaporated, but it calls for close attention. Caster, rather than granulated sugar is preferable, as the crystals are smaller and melt more quickly.

Sprinkle 200g caster sugar over the entire surface of a large, clean frying pan. Ideally the sugar should be no thicker than a few millimetres to ensure even colouring. Place the pan on a low to medium heat. The heat will start to melt the sugar at the edges, but leave it undisturbed. As more and more sugar melts and takes on colour, carefully swirl the pan to encourage even browning. You may need to use a fork to gently encourage the unmelted sugar to the outside of the pan to melt, but don't stir the sugar vigorously or it may crystallise. Eventually all the sugar should have melted and an even caramel formed. Act swiftly as the caramel will burn easily.

CARAMEL SAUCE

MAKES about 500ml

500g granulated sugar
500ml water

This results in a liquid caramel sauce, with the addition of water stopping the cooking of the caramel.

1 Put the sugar and 250ml of the water into a heavy-based saucepan. Place over a low heat and dissolve the sugar, using the handle of a wooden spoon to gently agitate the sugar to prevent it from 'caking' on the bottom of the saucepan. Try to avoid splashing syrup up the sides of the pan.

2 After brushing down the sides of the pan with a pastry brush dipped in water, bring the syrup to a gentle boil, without stirring, and boil until a deep golden brown colour. You may need to swirl the pan gently from time to time, but do not stir.

3 Immediately pour in the remaining 250ml water, taking care as the caramel will splutter and spit. Swirl the pan to dissolve the caramel and return it to a low heat, if necessary, until fully dissolved. Pour the caramel into a jug and cool until needed.

Variations

✳ **Lime caramel sauce** Once the remaining water has been added, stir through the finely grated zest and juice of 2 limes. Strain before use.

✳ **Spiced caramel sauce** Add to the finished caramel: 4 bay leaves, 4 star anise, 2 cinnamon sticks, 2 pared strips of lemon zest, 2 tbsp coriander seeds, crushed, and a 4cm piece of fresh root ginger, peeled and roughly chopped. Leave to infuse overnight and strain before use.

✳ **Butterscotch sauce** Make a caramel as for the main recipe but using 150g sugar and 4 tbsp water. When it reaches the desired caramel colour, add 150ml double cream, in place of the water, to stop the cooking. Stir well to dissolve, then stir in 30g unsalted butter.

CHOCOLATE SAUCE

MAKES 200ml

170g good quality dark
  chocolate
1 tsp instant espresso
  coffee powder

1 tsp boiling water
4 tbsp cold water
1 tbsp golden syrup
15g butter

1 Chop the chocolate into small pieces and put in a heatproof bowl set over a pan of just boiled water, ensuring the bowl is not touching the water. Give an occasional stir to help it melt.

2 Dissolve the coffee powder in the 1 tsp boiling water and allow to cool. Add to the melted chocolate with the remaining ingredients and stir until smooth and the sauce is shiny.

CRÈME ANGLAISE

MAKES 300ml

300ml whole milk
1 vanilla pod or a few drops
of vanilla extract

4 small or 3 large egg yolks
1–2 tbsp caster sugar

This classic custard, thickened with egg yolk, is served with all manner of puddings, including crumbles, pies and tarts. It is also the base for a classic ice cream. A good crème anglaise has the consistency of double cream and is thinner than a flour-thickened custard.

1 Put the milk in a saucepan. Cut the vanilla pod, if using, down one side, then scrape out all the seeds. Add the pod and seeds to the milk, place the pan over a medium heat and heat gently to scalding (see page 155). Just before it bubbles, take off the heat and remove the vanilla pod and any skin that has formed. Put the egg yolks and 1 tbsp of the sugar in a medium bowl and stir to mix. Pour in a little of the scalded milk and stir, then add the remaining milk gradually, stirring continuously until fully combined. Rinse out the saucepan used to scald the milk.

2 Return the milk and egg mixture to the cleaned pan. Place over a low to medium heat and stir continuously with a wooden spoon. First the custard will steam, which is an indication that it is about to thicken. Watch it carefully and keep stirring, getting the wooden spoon well into the corners.

3 To test if the sauce is thickened, remove it from the heat and draw the back of the spoon through the sauce. It should coat the back of the spoon evenly and not drop away and pool at the base of the spoon. When you draw a clean finger down the back of the spoon through the custard the trail should remain. This indicates that the sauce is ready.

4 When this point is reached, immediately strain the sauce through a chinois or fine sieve into a bowl. Taste and add more sugar if necessary. Set aside to cool. If you are using vanilla extract, add a few drops now.

5 To prevent a skin forming, place a disc of greaseproof paper on the crème anglaise, in direct contact with the surface.

Variations

✳ For a thicker crème anglaise, use all double cream in place of the milk, or half of each.

✳ **Crème anglaise with liqueur** Add ½–1 tbsp Calvados or Grand Marnier to the finished, thickened sauce.

✳ **Chocolate crème anglaise** Melt 30g chopped good quality dark chocolate in the milk when heating it. You may need to whisk the sauce to encourage the chocolate to melt fully.

✳ **Coffee crème anglaise** Substitute 30–50ml of the milk for a strong espresso.

A note on curdling...

A crème anglaise will curdle if the heat is too high. This occurs when the egg 'cooks' rather than thickens, resulting in flecks of cooked egg and causing the sauce to lose its velvety texture.

A note on undercooking...

If a crème anglaise is cooked at too low a temperature for too long, it will lose volume through water evaporation and develop a 'condensed milk' flavour.

1 Slowly stirring the hot milk into the egg yolks.

2 Stirring the custard continuously over a low to medium heat.

3 Drawing a finger down the back of the spoon to test if the sauce is thickened enough.

4 Straining the sauce through a chinois into a bowl.

THICK VANILLA CUSTARD

MAKES 250ml

450ml milk
2 egg yolks
60g caster sugar

30g plain flour, or
20g cornflour
Few drops of vanilla extract

Lovely with crumbles and steamed puddings, this is easier than crème anglaise, as the flour stops the egg from curdling. Use flour for a velvety texture, cornflour for a custard more like one made with custard powder.

1 Heat the milk to scalding point (see page 155). Put the egg yolks and sugar into a bowl and whisk together well. Add the flour and whisk again until smooth.

2 Pour the hot milk onto the yolk mixture, stirring as you do so, until well mixed. Rinse out the saucepan.

3 Return the mixture to the cleaned pan and bring slowly to the boil, stirring with a wooden spoon until thickened, less than 2 minutes. (Taste to check there is no raw flour flavour.) Add vanilla extract to taste, starting with 2 drops. Strain the custard through a sieve into a warmed jug for serving.

CRÈME PÂTISSIÈRE

MAKES 300ml

300ml whole milk
½ vanilla pod or a few drops
    of vanilla extract
3 egg yolks

50g caster sugar
15g plain flour
15g cornflour

Crème pâtissière, or pastry cream, is used as a sweet filling, in éclairs, roulades and millefeuille, for example.

1 Put the milk in a saucepan. Split the vanilla pod, if using, down one side, then scrape out the seeds. Add the pod and seeds to the milk and place the pan over a medium heat. Heat gently until steaming. Just before it bubbles, take off the heat and remove the vanilla pod and any skin that has formed.

2 Mix the egg yolks and sugar together in a medium bowl. Add a splash of the scalded milk, then the flours. Mix well, ensuring there are no lumps. Gradually stir in the remaining milk.

3 Return the mixture to a clean pan and place over a low to medium heat. Bring to the boil, stirring with a wooden spoon. It will go lumpy, but persevere and stir vigorously and it will become smooth. Turn the heat down and simmer for 2 minutes.

4 Remove from the heat and add the vanilla extract, if using. Transfer to a bowl and lay a disc of greaseproof paper on the surface, to prevent a skin forming. Set aside to cool.

5 Once cool, transfer the crème pâtissière to a food processor and blend until soft and smooth. It is now ready for use.

RASPBERRY COULIS

MAKES 250ml

50g granulated sugar
75ml water
250g raspberries (fresh
   or defrosted frozen ones)

Squeeze of lemon juice
   (optional)

1 Put the sugar and water into a saucepan. Place over a low heat and dissolve the sugar, using the handle of a wooden spoon to gently agitate the sugar to prevent it from 'caking' on the bottom of the saucepan (as shown on page 143). Try to avoid splashing syrup up the sides of the pan.

2 Once the sugar is dissolved, use a pastry brush dipped in water to brush down the sides of the pan (see page 143), to wash any remaining sugar crystals down into the syrup.

3 Turn the heat up, stop stirring from this point, and bring the syrup to the boil for 2 minutes, then remove from the heat and allow to cool slightly.

4 Put the raspberries into a food processor, pour on half the sugar syrup and blend to a purée.

5 Strain the coulis through a chinois or fine sieve into a bowl to remove the seeds.

6 Taste and adjust the consistency and sweetness with lemon juice or some of the remaining sugar syrup. The coulis should have a 'floodable' consistency.

Variations

✱ Any soft fruit can be used to make a coulis, such as strawberries and blueberries. Fruit juice, sugar syrup or water can be used to thin the sauce.

MELBA SAUCE

MAKES 200ml

250g fresh raspberries
30–50g icing sugar, to taste

This sauce can split on standing so it needs to be made shortly before serving.

1 Blend the raspberries and the icing sugar in a food processor until smooth, then pass through a fine sieve into a bowl.

2 Adjust the consistency of the sauce as required, with a little warm water and the sweetness with a little water and icing sugar combined.

TUILES

MAKES about 20

Oil, to grease
60g butter
2 large egg whites

125g caster sugar
60g plain flour
½ tsp vanilla extract

The tuile mixture can be stored in the fridge if you don't want to use it right away. We find the best way to make a stencil is to cut a shape in the lid of an empty ice-cream container, as the plastic is just the right thickness for the raw tuile mixture.

1 Heat the oven to 190°C/gas mark 5. Line 2 large baking sheets with pieces of baking parchment (use one for each tuile) and lightly oil a rolling pin. Put the butter into a small saucepan and melt over a low heat, then set aside to cool.

2 Put the egg whites into a bowl and, using a fork, beat in the sugar until just frothy. Sift in the flour, add the vanilla and combine well with a fork. Add the cooled, melted butter to the mixture and stir well. Chill for 10–15 minutes to firm the mixture a little, to make it easier to work with.

3 Using a round or triangular stencil, spread a spoonful of the mixture thinly into the desired shape on the prepared baking sheet, using a palette knife (as shown) or the back of a spoon. You need to bake the tuiles in batches of 4 at a time, to give you enough time to shape them before they cool down.

4 Bake in the oven for about 6 minutes until pale biscuit in colour in the middle and golden brown at the edges. Remove from the oven and leave to cool for a few seconds, to become pliable. Meanwhile, put a second batch in the oven on the second baking sheet.

5 Lift the cooked biscuits carefully off the baking sheet with a palette knife. Lay them, while still warm and pliable, over the rolling pin, to form them into a slightly curved shape (as shown). Once the shape has set, remove them carefully to a wire rack to cool.

6 Repeat with the remaining batches until the mixture is used up. The tuiles will keep for a few days, stored in an airtight container. Serve them as a contrasting accompaniment to ice creams or soft-textured dessert, such as mousses, soufflés and fruit fools, as a petit four.

A note on shaping the tuiles...

If the tuiles cool too much before shaping, return them to the oven for a few minutes to soften and make them pliable, but be aware that you cannot do this many times or they will eventually become very brittle and break very easily.

Variations

✱ Almond tuiles Scatter 30–40g flaked almonds over the tuiles before baking.

✱ Orange tuiles Stir the finely grated zest of ½ orange into the mixture with the flour and vanilla.

✱ Sesame tuiles Put 75g (about 3) egg whites into a medium bowl, crumble in 100g natural-coloured marzipan, sift in 55g plain flour and add 85g caster sugar. Beat the mixture using a hand-held electric whisk until smooth. Juice 1 lemon and add enough of the juice to the tuile mixture to form a smooth paste that is not too dry and not too runny; it should spread and hold. Stir in 2 tsp sesame seeds. Shape the mixture as for the main recipe and bake at 180°C/gas mark 4 for about 10 minutes, until pale golden brown. Shape the tuiles as for the main recipe. (Illustrated opposite.)

BRANDY SNAPS

MAKES 12–15

A little oil, to grease
100g butter
100g caster sugar
90g golden syrup

½ lemon
100g plain flour
Pinch of ground ginger

These round brandy snap biscuits can be shaped into baskets, tuiles or tubes that can be filled with cream.

1 Heat the oven to 190°C/gas mark 5. Line a baking sheet with baking parchment. Lightly oil any moulds you will need: the base of a timbale or jam jar for a basket, a rolling pin for a tuile or the handle of a wooden spoon for a tube.

2 Put the butter, sugar and syrup into a small saucepan, place over a low heat and stir until the sugar and butter have melted. Remove from the heat and leave to cool to room temperature. Squeeze the juice from the lemon and measure 1 tbsp.

3 Sift the flour and ginger into the cooled mixture (if too hot the mixture will turn lumpy) and stir well, then stir in the 1 tbsp lemon juice.

4 Place teaspoonfuls of the mixture on the prepared baking sheet, at least 10cm apart as they will spread out considerably.

You need to bake them in batches of 4 or 5 at a time; this will also give you time to shape them before they cool down. Bake in the oven for 5–7 minutes, or until the biscuits are an even, deep golden brown.

5 Remove from the oven and leave to set for just 30 seconds. Lift the biscuits from the baking sheet one at a time, using an oiled palette knife to prevent them sticking, onto a second oiled baking sheet for flat biscuits, or over your chosen mould, if shaping. Leave for a few minutes until just set on the moulds, then transfer to a wire rack to cool. You might need to warm the remaining brandy snaps in the oven to make them pliable again if they get too firm to mould.

6 Repeat with the remaining mixture, cooking and shaping in batches. Brandy snaps will keep for a few days, stored in an airtight container.

LANGUES DE CHAT

MAKES about 50	
100g butter, softened	3 egg whites
100g caster sugar	100g plain flour

These delicate biscuits, named 'cats' tongues' after their shape, are perfect to serve with ice creams, bavarois or mousses, to add a contrasting crisp texture.

1 Heat the oven to 200°C/gas mark 6. Line 2 or 3 large baking sheets with baking parchment.

2 Put the butter into a medium bowl and add about one third of the sugar. Cream together using a wooden spoon, then add the remaining sugar in 2 additions, beating until pale and fluffy.

3 Whisk the egg whites until frothy, then gradually mix into the creamed butter and sugar mixture using a spatula, beating well after each addition.

4 Sift in the flour and fold it in carefully with the spatula.

5 Spoon the mixture into a piping bag fitted with a 5–8mm plain nozzle. Pipe straight lines onto the prepared baking sheets, about 8cm long and the thickness of a pencil, spacing them well apart to allow room for spreading. Tap the baking sheets to release air bubbles from the mixture.

6 Bake in the oven for 5–8 minutes until the sponge biscuits are slightly risen and golden around the edges. Remove from the oven and leave to cool for a few seconds before carefully lifting the biscuits with a palette knife and transferring them to a wire rack to cool completely. They will keep for a few days, stored in an airtight container.

EQUIPMENT

Equipment

Trays and tins for baking do not need to be non-stick, but should be solid enough not to warp when they are heated.

Scales A set of good scales is imperative – electronic scales are more accurate when measuring smaller quantities

Chopping boards Separate board for raw and cooked foods

Bowls Various sizes, glass and/or stainless steel

Measuring jug

Juicer

Pie dishes Selection, including 1 litre

Pudding basin 850ml, 1 litre

Individual pudding basins 150ml

Dariole moulds 150ml

Jelly mould(s)

Cake tins Sandwich tins, springform tin, deep cake tin, Swiss roll tin

Loaf tin 450–500g

Loose-based flan tin

Baking sheets Some flat and some with a lip

Shallow baking tray

Roasting tin

Wire cooling rack

Oven gloves

Sugar thermometer

Utensils

Good kitchen tools make work in the kitchen easier and more efficient. The following are particularly useful when making desserts:

Measuring spoons

Wooden spoons

Slotted spoons

Basting spoon

Ladle

Fish slice

Rolling pin

Kitchen scissors (a sturdy pair)

Swivel vegetable peeler

Apple corer

Ice-cream scoop

Pastry cutters

Palette knife

Spatula (heat resistant)

Fine grater

Zester

Pans

Saucepans At least 3 in a range of sizes from 18–28cm

Frying pans At least 2 in different sizes, from 16–28cm

Knives

Large cook's knife Important for fine slicing, fine chopping and many other food preparation tasks

Paring knife For cutting small ingredients – to get close to them for more control

Pastry knife A long serrated knife used for cutting pastries, meringue desserts and cakes without crumbling or tearing

Small serrated knife This is very useful for preparing fruit

Small electrical equipment

Electric mixer (free standing) Perfect for mixing creamed cakes or whisking meringues

Hand-held electric whisk Creams together butter and sugar very swiftly. Also good for making meringues

Blender, Hand-held stick blender or Food processor For purées and coulis

Ice-cream machine For even-textured ice creams and sorbets

Paper/lining products

Greaseproof paper

Baking parchment/silicone paper

Aluminium foil

Cling film

Non-stick baking mats (re-usable)

GLOSSARY

ACIDULATED LIQUID Water with lemon juice or vinegar added, used to keep fruit such as pieces of apple from turning brown.

AGAR AGAR A vegetarian setting agent made from seaweed, used as an alternative to gelatine.

BAIN MARIE A hot water bath, often a roasting tin filled with water, used to protect a delicate dish from direct heat. Also used to keep food in a pan or bowl warm, such as a delicate sauce.

BALL STAGE, SOFT-/HARD Stages of sugar syrup boiling. To test, a little of the boiled syrup is dropped into cold water. At 115°C it will form a soft ball; at 120°C it will form a hard ball.

BOIL To cook food submerged in liquid heated so that the bubbles are constant and vigorous.

CARAMEL Sugar turned to a deep terracotta brown by heating.

CARAMELISE To bake (or roast or fry) to achieve colour and flavour as the natural sugars caramelise, such as the surface of a crème brûlée.

CARTOUCHE A circle of dampened greaseproof paper laid over fruit poaching under a lid, to keep the fruit immersed.

CHILL To cool food down in the fridge or using an ice bath, ideally to 4°C.

COULIS A thin purée, usually of fruit with a little sugar syrup.

CREAM To beat a mixture to incorporate air, typically butter and sugar for a cake.

CURDLE When an emulsion separates undesirably into solid and liquid, such as a curdled custard.

DROPPING CONSISTENCY When a mixture will drop reluctantly from a spoon if it is tapped on the side of the bowl or pan, neither pouring off nor continuing to stick to the spoon.

ENRICH To add cream, butter or a cream and egg yolk mixture to a sauce or other dish to thicken and enhance the flavour.

FLAMBÉ To set light to alcohol in a dish. A lit long match is held over the dish to ignite the alcohol, which is then burnt off as the liquid glazes the food, leaving a mellow flavour.

FLOOD THE PLATE To coat the base of a plate with sauce as part of the presentation. The sauce must be of a light, coating 'floodable' consistency.

FOLD To combine two or more mixtures using a large metal spoon or spatula and a lifting and turning motion to avoid losing air. Usually one mixture is more airy and delicate than the other.

GELATINE A setting agent for jellies and mousses available as thin sheets (leaves) or in powdered form, which must be fully dissolved. Made from animal bone/skin, it is not suitable for vegetarians but agar agar (see left) is a good alternative.

GLAZE To lend a glossy finish. For example, a jam glaze may be brushed over the fruit in a tart.

INFUSE To immerse aromatic ingredients such as herbs or spices in a hot liquid to flavour it.

LIGHTEN To incorporate air, by carefully folding egg whites or lightly whipped cream into a mixture for example.

LOOSEN When combining whisked egg whites into a heavier mixture, to first stir in a spoonful of the whisked whites before folding in the rest.

MACERATE To soak food, usually fruit, in a flavoured liquid, sometimes containing alcohol, to soften it and allow the exchange of flavour.

MOUSSE A sweet (or savoury) dish, where the air bubbles from whisked egg whites (and also usually cream), make the texture frothy and light.

NEEDLESHREDS Finely and evenly cut shreds of citrus zest, typically used as a decoration.

PANADE The thick base mixture of a soufflé or choux pastry. Made from butter, flour and milk or water, it is also used as a binding mixture.

PINCH An approximate quantity that can be pinched between the thumb and forefinger, less than ⅛ tsp.

PITH The soft white layer directly beneath the coloured zest of citrus fruit. It is invariably bitter in flavour and avoided when zesting the fruit.

POACH To submerge food in liquid that is hot yet barely trembling (certainly not bubbling), either on the hob or in the oven.

PURÉE Usually fruit or vegetables, blended and/or sieved until smooth.

REDUCE To rapidly boil a liquid, such as a sauce, to concentrate the flavour by evaporation.

RELAX OR REST To leave pastry in a cool place, to allow the gluten to relax before baking and minimise shrinkage in the oven. Batters are also left to rest before use to allow the starch cells to swell, which results in a lighter cooked result.

RIBBON STAGE When a whisked egg or mousse mixture is thick enough to leave a line or ribbon over the surface when the whisk is lifted and some of the mixture falls from it.

ROAST To cook uncovered, without added liquid, in the oven.

RUB IN To rub small pieces of butter into flour with the fingertips until the mixture resembles breadcrumbs, as for pastry or a crumble topping.

SCALD To heat a liquid (milk, usually) until on the verge of boiling. At scalding point, steam is escaping and bubbles are starting to form around the edge of the pan.

SEASON Usually simply to flavour with salt and pepper, but it can also involve adjusting acidity with lemon juice or sweetness by adding sugar.

SIMMER To cook food submerged in liquid, heated to a level that ensures small bubbles constantly appear around the edge of the pan.

SLAKE To blend a thickening ingredient such as cornflour with a little cold water, before mixing into the sauce to thicken it. Unstable ingredients such as yoghurt should also be slaked into a mixture using a little of the sauce, to prevent curdling.

SPONGE Soaking powdered gelatine in a little water until it forms a translucent spongy gel before melting.

STEAM To cook food gently in hot vapour, usually from boiling water. The food is placed in a perforated container and cooks in the steam that surrounds it. A steamed pudding is cooked by indirect steaming: the food is protected from the steam itself but cooks in the heat created by it.

SYRUPY The consistency of a sauce reduced down until it just coats the back of a spoon. Similar to warm syrup or honey.

THREAD STAGE An early stage of sugar syrup boiling. To test, a little of the boiled sugar syrup is dropped into cold water, then removed and pulled between the finger and thumb. At 110°C it will form a fine thread as it is pulled.

ZEST The coloured outer skin of citrus fruit, used for flavouring. 'To zest' finely pare the zest, avoiding the bitter white pith, using a zester.

INDEX

ACKNOWLEDGEMENTS

The recipes in this book have been compiled, adapted and edited by Jenny Stringer, Claire Macdonald and Camilla Schneideman, but the authors are a large collection of Leiths staff and visiting teachers, past and present. Thank you to everyone who wrote recipes for this book, notably: Claire Macdonald, Max Clark, Heli Miles, Jess Mills, Shenley Moore, Sue Nixon, Camilla Schneideman, Jenny Stringer, Ron Sweetser and Priya Wickramasinghe.

But with the sheer number of talented cooks around us at the school, we must say a big thank you to everyone who has helped develop ideas for this book, tested the recipes (particularly Sarah Hall who undertook an intensive testing programme!) and given valuable feedback during the tasting sessions. Special thanks must go to Helene Robinson-Moltke, Ansobe Smal and Belinda Spinney who were at the photo shoots.

Thank you to the team at Quadrille. We have been extremely lucky to continue our relationship with our editor Janet Illsley. Janet's patience with the authors is legendary – deadlines with this number of people involved required military organisation and, as ever, we are incredibly grateful for her wisdom. Thank you too Sally Somers for editing the copy.

Thank you to the team that worked together on the design and photography for this book: Peter Cassidy for his brilliant photography, Gabriella Le Grazie for her art direction, Emily Kydd and Emily Quah (both Leiths graduates) for the food styling. We are thrilled with the new style Katherine Keeble has created for this series of books, so thank you all.

CREATIVE DIRECTOR Helen Lewis
PROJECT EDITOR Janet Illsley
DESIGN Katherine Keeble
ART DIRECTION Gabriella Le Grazie
PHOTOGRAPHER Peter Cassidy
FOOD STYLISTS Emily Kydd and Emily Quah
LEITHS CONSULTANTS Helene Robinson-Moltke, Ansobe Smal and Belinda Spinney
COPY EDITOR Sally Somers
PROPS STYLISTS Iris Bromet and Cynthia Inions
PRODUCTION Vincent Smith, Tom Moore

First published in 2015 by
Quadrille Publishing Limited
www.quadrille.co.uk

Cataloguing in Publication Data: a catalogue record for this book is available from the British Library.

ISBN 978 184949 5509

Printed in China